Richard Hooker Wilmer

**The Old Flag**

Richard Hooker Wilmer

**The Old Flag**

ISBN/EAN: 9783337091774

Printed in Europe, USA, Canada, Australia, Japan

Cover: Foto ©ninafisch / pixelio.de

More available books at **www.hansebooks.com**

# THE
# OLD FLAG.

True to thy God,—thou canst not then be false
To man, nor traitor to thy country prove,—
Most loyal, if thy loyalty have root
In love for Heaven, for Freedom and the Right.

PHILADELPHIA:
AMERICAN SUNDAY-SCHOOL UNION,
No. 1122 CHESTNUT STREET.

NEW YORK: 599 BROADWAY.

Entered, according to Act of Congress, in the year 1864, by the
AMERICAN SUNDAY-SCHOOL UNION,
in the Clerk's Office of the District Court of the United States
for the Eastern District of Pennsylvania.

# CONTENTS.

### CHAPTER I.
A July Morning.................................................... 7

### CHAPTER II.
The Tea-Party.................................................... 18

### CHAPTER III.
Family History................................................... 27

### CHAPTER IV.
The Patriot...................................................... 43

### CHAPTER V.
A Day in School.................................................. 58

### CHAPTER VI.
The Fishing-Party................................................ 78

### CHAPTER VII.
The Decision..................................................... 91

### CHAPTER VIII.
Sunday in the Red House.......................................... 110

### CHAPTER IX.
Sunday Evening................................................... 125

### CHAPTER X.
The Town-Meeting................................................. 139

### CHAPTER XI.
Sleep............................................................ 154

## CONTENTS.

### CHAPTER XII.
Ten Years Later.................................................. 160

### CHAPTER XIII.
The Wood-Lot.................................................... 175

### CHAPTER XIV.
The Birthday..................................................... 190

### CHAPTER XV.
Voting............................................................ 199

### CHAPTER XVI.
Eighteen Hundred and Sixty.................................... 216

### CHAPTER XVII.
The Great Question............................................. 229

### CHAPTER XVIII.
Loyalty........................................................... 248

### CHAPTER XIX.
A Talk with Susan............................................... 262

### CHAPTER XX.
Volunteering..................................................... 270

### CHAPTER XXI.
The New Captain................................................ 292

### CHAPTER XXII.
Army Letters..................................................... 307

### CHAPTER XXIII.
Battle of Fredericksburg....................................... 324

### CHAPTER XXIV.
A Surprise........................................................ 338

### CHAPTER XXV.
The Parting...................................................... 360

# THE OLD FLAG.

## CHAPTER I.

### A JULY MORNING.

I WISH to take my reader back to the year 1840, and introduce him to a family which was then living in the western part of the State of Connecticut. To reach them, we must leave the travelled road leading from the Connecticut River to the Hudson, and strike northward among the hills which abound in that portion of the State. Among these hills the soil was sterile and rocky, and only partially brought under cultivation, large tracts still lying in woodland and pasturage. There was a sparse population scattered here and there on the high points, or in the sheltered valleys between the hills, living a primitive, laborious life. On descending a steep abrupt hill, there came in view a small farm, which attracted notice from being in so high a state of cultivation. It had several acres in corn, and several more in rye and wheat,—the latter waving in the bright sunshine, and just beginning to turn from its original blue-green to the golden tint which foretells a speedy ripening. On the opposite side of the road there was a meadow, where labourers were at work, and from which was sent forth far and near the delicious fragrance of newly-mown grass.

The house belonging to this farm was small, having but one story, and standing half-way down the hill. It faced the east, and was painted a bright red, with door and window-facings of white. In front of it stood two large chestnut-trees, overhanging the low roof and sheltering it from the sun. The barn, considerably larger than the house, was surmounted by a curious weather-vane,—a miniature ship, with masts and rigging all complete, with a rudely-carved figure-head, whose extended finger was supposed to indicate the direction of the wind. There was attached to this a weather-beaten flag, whose broad stripes floated forth on the freshening breeze, now and then giving a loud, joyful snap as the wind stretched it out to its full extent. Another tiny flag was elevated on the gate-post, reminding the passer-by, if the ringing bells had not before brought the fact to his mind, that it was the Fourth of July,—or Independence Day, as they called it here.

By following the only trodden path, the back door was reached. It opened into a large, unfinished room, whose doors and windows were all open to admit the air,— a room which was used by the family in summer as a kitchen, though it was only a kind of shed-room. It was very clean;

and in it, with arms bared to the elbow, stood the mother of the family, busily engaged in making up rolls of rich, golden-looking butter.

The family living in this cottage consisted of Mr. Roberts, a middle-aged man, his wife, two daughters of fourteen and sixteen, and two sons, one ten years old and the other only five. Last, but by no means least in the estimation of the others, was Grandfather Roberts, or Captain Roberts, as the neighbours called him, an old sea-captain, nearly eighty years of age, though still hale and hearty.

Mrs. Roberts, a plain, sensible-looking woman, carried her butter into the cellar, and, after washing the dishes, she drew from the oven a huge loaf of cake and commenced frosting it. It was nearly covered with a thick, glittering coat of sugar, when some one exclaimed, "Oh, mother, how nice it looks! I do believe it will be the handsomest loaf there! And just see what beautiful lilies I have got!

This tall stalk shall stand up in the middle, and I'll put a wreath of myrtle and roses round it. Oh, won't it be beautiful, mother?"

Mrs. Roberts smiled as she looked at the beaming face of her youngest daughter, who was standing with her apron full of flowers, and a magnificent bunch of white lilies in her hand. The loaf thus ornamented was for a picnic, or, as they called it in that primitive place, a *tea-party*, which was to be held in a grove near the centre of Woodlee, in honour of the day.

"Yes, it will be very pretty, Lucy. But we mustn't forget other things, if it is Independence. The men will be at home a little earlier to dinner; for grandfather says they mustn't be cheated out of a good, plump half-day's frolic; and Sam and Abner must both go home and dress themselves after dinner."

"Are they going to the party?"

"Yes, of course: there won't be a

young man, woman or child staying at home such a day as this. Sam says his mother has made a pailful of doughnuts and three strawberry pies to carry."

"I hope I sha'n't have to eat any of them,—such a dirty-looking hole as their kitchen is," said Lucy, with a shrug.

"Hush, Lucy! Will you never learn to say only what is kind of others? But you mustn't make that wreath now. There are potatoes to pare, and it's high time the water was on to boil them; and you must pick the lettuce,—it ought to be in cold water freshening this very minute,—and then you'd better run over into the pasture and pick a bowlful of strawberries; grandfather thinks every thing of strawberries and milk, you know."

"Why, I sha'n't have a bit of time to make my wreath; and I want to make another one to wear on my head, and I must baste the lace into my muslin frock, and——"

"*And* there is plenty of time for it all,

if you don't stand here fretting. Mabel and I will wash the dishes and do all the after-dinner work, and two o'clock will be quite early enough to start."

So the flowers were laid in a basin of water, the lettuce gathered, and its broad curly leaves plunged into cold water to make them cool and crisp; then the ever-active Lucy ran over to the pasture, skipped over the bars, and in less than twenty minutes was back again by her mother's side, with a heated face, and a quart bowl filled with delicious strawberries.

"Go in, now, and set the table, Lucy; I'll pick over the strawberries. But just put up the fire under the kettle, and see if the flat-iron is hot: I promised Mabel to smooth out her dress."

So it was all stir and animation in the Roberts's kitchen till dinner-time, when four stout hungry men sat down to a genuine farmer's dinner, such as was then and is now, common in all New-England farm-houses, composed of boiled pork and corned beef, with turnips and potatoes, and ending with a boiled Indian-pudding. Prepared by "the very neat-handed" Mrs. Roberts, it was a meal not to be despised; for the beef was of the tenderest kind, of a bright rose colour streaked with white, the vegetables boiled just enough to preserve their sweetness, the bread light and wholesome, the butter like pure gold, with the delicious flavour of green pastures pervading it, and the pudding light and tender, with rich maple-syrup and cream poured abundantly over it. Yes, it was a dinner fit for a king, not to say for those four independent American farmers, each of whom sitting there in his shirt-sleeves considered himself equal, if not a peg or two superior, to any king who ever sat on a throne.

Before the meal was finished, the other members of the family had returned; Mabel from a busy forenoon's work of arranging with others the tables for the party, and Leonard and Sydney from school; for in those days boys had only a half-holiday even on the Fourth of July. They burst into the room ravenous with hunger and boiling over with excitement.

"I say, father," shouted Leonard, "the down-town boys are going to get out the big cannon to-night and fire it off as many times as there are States. Won't it make a big noise!"

"Oh, do be careful, or you'll get hurt, boys," said the anxious mother. But the words were scarcely heard by the excited boys.

"And oh, father, mayn't I get some powder with the ten cents you gave me?"

"Spend it as you please; only be careful if you have powder about," replied his father.

"And be sure and not let Sydney go near it," added the mother: "there are always so many accidents, I do dread to have Independence come."

"Oh, don't make cowards of the boys, mother," said grandfather. "A little smell of powder never hurt a Yankee shaver."

Leonard considered this sound doctrine, and could hardly wait to be dressed in his Sunday-clothes before he started off to make the desired investment; while Sydney remained behind, it having been decided, much to his disgust, that it was more prudent to have him under his mother's care, who at the moment was trying to reduce his rebellious, sandy curls into something like order,—no easy task, with his restless head bobbing about incessantly.

But at length all were ready. The wreaths had been made, the loaf of cake trimmed to the general admiration of the family and sent on by Abner, the work done up, the house put in order, the two girls dressed in pretty white muslins and the mother in her black silk; and when the latter, with grandfather and little Sydney,—the last to leave,—walked out by the little footpath and shut the gate, the farm-house was utterly deserted, save by the sober-minded cat, who sat washing her face on the door-step as demurely as if the Independence of these United States of America had never been declared.

## CHAPTER II.

### THE TEA-PARTY.

It was a pleasant sight to see the people who had collected on the green in Woodlee that summer afternoon,—some coming on horseback, some in wagons, some on foot, old men and young, matrons and maidens, children and babies, all arrayed in their best, and prepared to make that one half-day at least a season of joyful festivity. The first exercise of the occasion was an oration in the church, to be delivered by the Hon. James Bailey, the one lawyer of Woodlee, who had been twice elected to the Legislature, and once had even attained to the honour of being one of the Governor's Council. Of course Woodlee was proud of him; and when he read the Declaration of Independence in a full, sonorous voice, every eye was fixed on him in admiration. If, in the long, loudly-spoken address which followed, there were more gorgeous metaphors, and more grandiloquent assertions of the superiority of this mighty American Republic over all the nations that ever did or ever will exist, than was consistent with good taste, nobody in that audience was troubled by it. And when the good pastor followed with a fervent supplication to Almighty God that their liberties might be preserved to them and to their children's children to the latest generation, and the choir sung a patriotic hymn, every heart in the assembly beat with a prouder consciousness that to be a citizen of these United States was something to rejoice in and be thankful for.

After leaving the church, the people adjourned to the grove, where the long tables, bountifully filled, and glowing with bright flowers, were set, and already surrounded by laughing maidens, whose blue sashes and flower-wreaths proclaimed them the presiding spirits of the scene. Among these one would scarcely fail to mark Mabel Roberts, a tidy, pure-complexioned, neatly-dressed lassie, whose snowy muslin robe and garland of flowers became her well;—at least so thought her mother, as she watched her movements with a calm, fond eye.

Many of the old people returned home from the church; but more remained and gathered themselves in knots at a little distance from the tables, where some board seats had been laid, to talk over the news of the day, or of the old times, which to them seemed so much better than the present. Among these the young folks flitted about, dispensing refreshments, or eating them with jokes and noisy laughter. 'Twas a bright, merry scene, none the less joyful that it was all thoroughly country-like, and to a fastidious eye might have lacked somewhat of refinement and elegance. There were doughnuts and cheese, and pies and pickles to be eaten, and the vases of flowers were in some cases composed of peonies and other blossoms larger and higher-coloured than was agreeable to the most cultivated taste; but no city assembly ever contained a larger proportion of innocent, honest, happy hearts.

There were more speeches at the table: a short one from the minister; a funny one from the doctor; and then, to everybody's astonishment, Grandfather Roberts rose, his tall form a little bowed and trembling, and his left hand raised to stroke back the gray locks from his forehead.

"You all know I ain't used to makin' speeches," he said, in a hearty, natural voice, "but somehow since I've been settin' here lookin' at these boys and girls, and seein' how happy they all feel, and then lookin' up at that flag hangin' over their heads, I felt as if I must say a word or two. I'm an old man, and very likely this is the last Independence I shall ever see: so you must have patience if I don't call all my words jist as young folks do.

The boys all like to see that flag: they love to look at the bright colours, and the stripes and stars, but they don't know but little about what it really means. *I* know —yes, *I* know," and he straightened himself up as he said it; "for I've fought under it. I know how a sight of that are flag hangin' at the mast-head makes a sailor's heart spring and his eye shine when cannon-balls are flyin' all round him, and how he'd rather die then hev it lowered, —yes, die a thousand times over then to see it topple down and an enemy's run up instead! I fought under Commodore Perry on the lakes, when the Britishers wanted to lord it over our sailors and to carry 'em off jist when they pleased, to sarve aboard their men-o'-war. We jist showed 'em how to let us alone in future; that's what we did!

"But it warn't of that, nor 'bout myself, that I got up to talk. I say these boys don't know what that flag means, nor what it means to have a country. Our forefathers, who are dead and gone, knew; for they bought it for us by fightin', and dyin', and sufferin' all kinds of privations and hardships: they bought a country where everybody's rights are protected, and nobody can interfere to wrong or harm us, by sheddin' their blood like water; but we jist sit down here at our ease and enjoy it, and think it's allers goin' to last and nobody have any trouble. Perhaps 'twill. I hope 'twill. It does seem as if things are all fixed now so they'll go right along slick and easy; but nobody knows for sartain. So I want, boys, you should remember two things. One is, that you've got a country that cost somethin', and is worth somethin'; and the other is, that you ought to love this country better then any thing else in the whole world. Lovin' our country means somethin' besides firin' cannon and makin' speeches Fourth of Julys, tho' them's all well enough: it means understandin' what it's worth to us, and bein' willin' to give up every thing for it,—even our very lives, if it's ever necessary. You all laugh to hear me say that, 'cause you are so sure it never will be necessary. Mabbe 'twon't; but didn't you never see the sky in the mornin' so blue and clear there wan't a speck of a cloud on it as big as your finger-nail, and then hev a black cloud come right up sudden, and the wind a blowin' great guns, and the water a foamin' and pitchin' like mad, afore night, and the sky a lookin' as if it never was a shinin' blue and never would be? Now, I hain't much larnin', but I've read a little, and I know the nations of the airth are allers gettin' into trouble; and mabbe we can't expect to be better off then they. So, for all the sky looks so smilin' now, it may be black and squally before you die. Any way, it won't do no harm to keep your sails reefed a bit, and a taut hold on the helm. People never keep their libbaty long if they don't desarve it; and if we git proud and wicked, and sot up in our own eyes, and forget the God who helped us, we sha'n't be fit for freedom, and then it will be took away from us. Sometimes I think these young folks may live to see the day when they'll have to buy their libbaties over again, and pay the price,— may live to see the old flag a wavin' agin over battle-fields and dyin' men. God forbid! and perhaps 'tain't likely. But then I do want every boy here to grow up a lovin' his country so well that, if ever he should be called to it, he will follow that dear blessed flag, that's floatin' up there agin the sunshine, right into the hottest fight, as brave as Washington himself. That's all I've got to say. Love God; do your duty to him fust, and then you'll allers be ready to do your duty to everybody else; and be sartain to do it to the dear blessed country God has given to you to keep as long as you live and then leave for your children after you."

Tears were falling down the old man's

face when he sat down. Other hearts, too, were touched, and other eyes were tearful; for all knew that the speaker had been a brave man, and a true lover of his country.

## CHAPTER III.

### FAMILY HISTORY.

"Didn't grandfather talk first-rate yesterday?" asked Leonard Roberts the next morning.

"Yes," answered his mother, smiling.

"I felt sorry, though, when he first got up," said Lucy; "for he talks so old-fashioned, I thought they would all laugh at him."

"You never need feel ashamed of your grandfather, Lucy," said Mrs. Roberts, with a slight shade of displeasure in her voice: "his age and sound good sense will always command respect from those whose opinion is of any value, even if a few silly boys should laugh at his pronunciation."

"Mr. Granby said" (Mr. Granby was

the minister) "that he was the best man in town to make a Fourth-of-July speech," said Leonard, "because he was a true patriot. What is a true patriot, mother?"

"Ask your grandfather, Leonard: I am too busy to explain it just now. Besides, he can do it better than I."

"But he's off in the lot, working at the hay. Oh, I wish I could stay at home from school and turn hay! It's real fun!"

"I dare say; but I think your grandfather will tell you one of the things necessary for a true patriot is to lay the foundation for a good education now you are young and have the time for it."

"Ho! A patriot don't mean *that!* I know," said Leonard, contemptuously. "It means fighting, or being brave, or something of that sort. But I shall ask grandfather when I get home: he'll tell me all about it."

With this resolve, Leonard went to look for Sydney, whose morning-hours were usually divided between two white pigs

"The two boys set off down the hill, with their dinner pail in hand."

p. 29.

in the pen, and four broods of chickens, whose mothers were shut up in coops in the yard, while the chickens ran about among the grass, and had become so tame and well acquainted with the little fellow that he could take them up in his hand at any time. He usually rebelled a little at being summoned to prepare for school; and the daily ordeal of having his hands and face washed, his hair combed and a clean apron put on, was evidently considered by him a most severe affliction.

When it was over, the two boys set off down the hill, with their tin dinner-pail in hand. They had a walk of three-quarters of a mile to take; and, as they went leisurely along the road, coarsely but cleanly dressed, with bare feet and sun-browned faces, they were fair representatives of the sons of our New England farmers in that day.

Leonard was rather short and thick-set, with broad, square shoulders. His eyes were dark gray, his hair brown, and his features large,—especially his nose and mouth. He would, no doubt, be called a plain-looking boy: still, he had a sensible face, and a frank open expression somewhat redeemed its plainness. Sydney was a homely boy, too, but of a different type. His abundant locks decidedly inclined to red, and he was freckled; his eyes were of a light blue, his lips delicate and finely cut, and his whole face indicated a far more sensitive nature than Leonard's; he was more slenderly built, too, and looked delicate, while Leonard was the very picture of rude health and vigour. While they proceed on their way to school, we will give some details of the family history.

Old Mr. Roberts—or Captain Roberts, as he was usually called—was born on the island of Nantucket, and, like most boys born there, he early went to sea, and followed the seas for many years,—sometimes going on merchant-vessels, but oftener on whaling-voyages. This mode of life made him (almost of course) hardy, bold and adventurous; and, what was not so common, he also became a temperate, upright, God-fearing man. In time he married, remaining at home for two years afterwards; but he pined to be once more on the sea, and, having risen to be second mate of a whaler, he went several long voyages in that capacity, rarely returning oftener than once in three years, and remaining only two or three months at longest. In time he became first mate, and then master, of a vessel. On the breaking out of the War of 1812, fired with indignation at what he considered the violation by Great Britain of the rights of American seamen, he enlisted in the naval service of the United States, and was a most brave and efficient officer, first in the Mediterranean Squadron, and afterwards under Commodore Perry in his brilliant career on the lakes.

At the close of the war, being somewhat disabled by the injuries he had received, and past forty years of age, he decided to retire from the sea and purchase a farm, where his sons might be trained to a life of less hardship and peril than his own had been. So he emigrated to the State of Connecticut with a wife and four children, and settled in the little town of Woodlee, building there the small cottage in which we find him. There his wife and one son had died, there his two daughters had married, and there he was now spending a green old age with his only surviving son, who, being born on the same day on which Washington died, he had named George Washington.

Perhaps the strongest trait in the character of the old sea-captain was his intense love of the flag under which he had served, and which he regarded with a veneration and homage only second to that he felt for his Bible and God. To him that strip of bunting represented the country he loved, the country for which he had perilled life and limb. Its stripes were symbols of the precious blood shed in its defence, and its stars, of the crowns the brave heroes who had fought on her battlefields had won. Every Fourth of July, whether in sunshine or in storm, he unrolled it to the breeze; and never could he look at it, as it floated forth, without deep emotion, so significant was it to him of all that was dearest to him as a citizen of a free nation. In his mind, love of God and love of country were never dissevered, the latter growing out of the former as naturally as the fruit from the stalk.

"Talk of a man's being loyal to God and disloyal to his country!" he would sometimes say: "why, it ain't nateral to think of such a thing. If a man loves God, he does the things God wants him to; and don't he want him to sarve his country? Who but God gave him such a country as this, and blessed it,—a country where every man sits in his own house in safety and worships God after his own conscience, with nobody to molest or make afraid? And if anybody in these United

States ain't grateful to God for the privileges he has given to him, and don't do all he can to be worthy of 'em, then he don't desarve to have such privileges: that's all!"

It was a favourite habit of his to talk to Leonard about the flag, and how much blood had been shed to protect it; and he would often wind up by saying,—

"Now, boy, I tell you, if anybody ain't willing to shed the last drop of his blood to keep that old flag a flyin', he's too mean a coward to live in a free country: he ought to go and live among the Britishers and put his neck right under the heel of the old despot."

Sensible and pious as the old captain was, he had an intense hatred of the British, and never was willing to believe that, next to his own land, England was the nation of all others in the world where the civil and religious rights of the inhabitants were best secured. He could only remember the cruel treatment our seamen had received at her hands, and that they had fired on our flag and tried to lay it in the dust.

After Independence Day had passed, the flag was taken down and carefully laid away, with the injunction, "Now, mind, children, if grandfather ain't here, don't forget to set the old flag a wavin' on the Fourth : 'pears to me 'twould do me good to see it, even in another world."

George Washington Roberts had inherited much of his father's patriotic feeling, but he was of a less enthusiastic temperament, being a quiet, reserved man, of thorough integrity, but inclined to take rather gloomy views of life. His experience had not been of a nature to overcome this natural distrust. The farm, bought when he was a young man and at that time lying chiefly in woodland, with only a little clearing round the house, had been brought under excellent cultivation, principally by his own efforts. He had toiled early and late, lived frugally, and denied himself in all ways, that the farm might be made a valuable possession for himself and his children; and a valuable possession it became, giving abundant proof of the industry and thrift of its owner. Where the forest had stood, there were now acres of choice pasturage, and other acres of fine mowing; while others still, glowed with harvests of golden grain.

But in an evil hour George and his father set their names to a note of hand as endorsers for a wealthy merchant in the place. The wealthy merchant absconded within a year, leaving nearly everybody in the country involved in his ruin; for his reputation had been such that every person who had a little money to invest was sure to place it in his hands; and execrations deep, if not loud, were breathed upon the defaulter by many a poor widow and orphan whose little all had been swallowed up.

To meet the demands for money thus pressing upon them, the two Roberts were compelled to sell a large portion of their beautiful farm, and to mortgage the remainder; and five years after, when our little narrative commences, this mortgage still remained, though a small payment had been made each year. To do this, and support the family on the small farm left, required the most rigid economy; and this was practised, every household arrangement being made in reference to one great end,—paying off the debt.

Notwithstanding this economy, there was an air of neatness and comfort pervading the red house which would have astonished one not familiar with the resources of a capable Yankee housekeeper; —and an excellent housekeeper Mrs. Roberts certainly was, in every sense of the word. She knew where to curtail expense and where to be liberal, knowing that to scrimp in some places was only a false economy, tending to poverty and not to thrift. Her children, though always dressed in the plainest manner (her daughters' white muslins, pretty but inexpensive garments, being all the dresses they had, except the plainest for every-day wear), were never kept at home from school; and books, maps, and whatever was necessary to their progress while there, were freely provided. Rich cake and pastry were unknown in the house; but in the sitting-room there was a little shelf of books, containing some valuable histories and works of travel. In short, Mary Roberts, plain, unpretending woman as she was, had learned (what some better-educated people never do) that what nourishes the mind and conduces to its growth is of more value to a child than what tickles the palate; though, like all really good housekeepers, she was careful to provide a supply of wholesome, well-cooked food for the family, and, indeed, rather prided herself on having nicer bread, butter and cheese than most of her neighbours.

But it was all the product of their own

land. They raised their own beef and pork, their grain and vegetables, their milk, butter and cheese, and even made their sugar and molasses from the maple-trees which grew on the hill opposite the house. And, as only grandfather drank tea or coffee, there was very little outlay for the table. Indeed, it is a misuse of the term to speak of poverty in a New-England farm-house where there is any thing like thrifty management and where intemperance has never gained a foothold. What greater luxuries could any table boast than were furnished by that nice garden which the old gentleman took care of, with Leonard's help,—whose little fingers were early taught to weed the beds,—and which was sure to yield such radishes and lettuce, such peas, beans and corn, as grew in few other gardens, because grandfather was so very nice and particular about planting and weeding them? When freshly gathered and nicely cooked, they were indeed delicious; so were the rich milk and cream, and the berries which grew wild in every pasture around them, and could always be had in their season for the gathering.

The farm yielded, in addition, fuel (for a portion of it was still uncleared), and pasturage for a flock of sheep, from which they got not only wool enough to make winter-garments, but quite an overplus to sell to the wool-dealers of a neighbouring county. Their wool and butter were their principal sources of income; for, though they raised considerable grain and hay, most of it was consumed on the farm in the winter months, and the larger proportion of the farm was better adapted to grazing than to tillage.

The garden gave them another luxury, —flowers; for the girls, with now and then a little help from their grandfather, cultivated the borders, and in summer and autumn they bloomed out into a profusion of peonies, roses, lilies, pinks, marigolds, and other old-fashioned flowers which it did a body's heart good to look at,—to say nothing of the sage and sweet-marjoram, and wormwood, hoarhound and rue, which also grew there to season their sausages and cure their coughs and colds.

So, in spite of the debt, and the economy they were obliged to use, the dwellers in the snug farm-house had many enjoyments, and a spirit of contentment and peace reigned throughout their little domain.

A very small domain it was, so far as the house itself was concerned; for it had been originally intended only for the kitchen-part, before which a larger front part was to be erected; and the preparations for this new part were all made when the debt came upon them; but now it was indefinitely postponed. So that it was a mere box of a dwelling, scarcely larger than a marten's box. There were only two rooms of any size in it, the front one being the "best room;" the other served for sitting-room, dining-room, and also kitchen, except in summer, when the cooking-stove was taken out into the unfinished room in the back shed. Out of these two rooms doors opened into two tiny bedrooms, each just large enough for a bed, washstand and chair; and up-stairs were two attic rooms, where the children slept.

Every part of this little dwelling was as neat as wax; and this neatness and order gave a charm to it sometimes wanting in houses of larger dimensions. Indeed, both the parents and children were sincerely attached to this humble dwelling, and seldom felt a wish for one more elegant or imposing. It is love and kindness which make home the cherished place, or, in the words of the good old proverb, make it "home, be it ever so homely;" and to its inmates the red house was indeed a home in the best sense of that expressive word.

## CHAPTER IV.

### THE PATRIOT.

It was not till after he had eaten his bread-and-milk that night, that Leonard found his grandfather sufficiently at leisure to answer his question. Then, as the old gentleman was sitting in the door to enjoy the evening breeze, he came and sat down by him.

"I want to know what a patriot means, grandfather. Mother said you could tell me better than anybody."

"A patriot? A patriot? Why, it's a man who loves his country with all his heart."

"But doesn't it mean a man who fights for it?"

"Yes, if it's necessary he'll fight for it, of course; but a true patriot is the man who does all he can for his country in just such times as he happens to live in, whether they're war-times or peace-times. Some patriots have saved their country by dyin' on battle-fields, some by makin' good laws for it, some by standin' up agin oppression, and bein' parsecuted, and put in prison, and may-be hung, because they wouldn't submit to tyranny and wrong. This, I take it, is the toughest kind of patriotism; for 'tain't no mighty matter, when a man's blood is up, to go into battle and be shot; but it must be tryin' to lie in prison, and be hung on a gallows, like a thief or murderer. Yes, there's a sight of ways by which a man can do something for his country if he wants to; and if he truly sarves it in any way, he's a patriot."

Then came out, rather hesitatingly, the question which had been stirring in the boy's mind:—"Can *I* be a patriot, grandfather?"

"Why, God bless you, yes, boy! there ain't nothin' to hender your growin' up as good a patriot as ever breathed." After a little pause, he added, "And the sooner you begin about it, the better."

Leonard opened his eyes. Probably visions of flashing more powder and firing heavier cannon, danced through his brain.

"You ought to be beginnin' now; because if a boy don't start right he ain't apt to come out right. If he begins by disobeyin' his parents, cheatin' other boys, and doin' all sorts of mean, dirty tricks and thinkin' they're smart and cunnin', he's amazin' apt to end in bein' a low, good-for-nothin' fellow, a disgrace to himself and his country both. Now, nobody can be a patriot who ain't honest, and who don't tell the truth let it cost what it will. So, if you begin now to despise all low, mean, vulgar tricks, and to stand up for the truth without flinchin' a hair if you do have to suffer for it, you'll be layin' the foundation for a patriot; because a patriot is an honest man and a brave man,—whereas a liar is never any thing but a poor, cowardly sneak of a critter all his life.

"Yes, as I was sayin', there's a great many ways, Leonard, of doin' something for your country; and some are called to do one thing, and some another. I don't know as you are old enough to understand about such things yet; but when you get older your old grandfather may-be won't be here to talk with you."

"Oh, yes, I can understand, grandfather. Why, I'm ten years old next November!"

"Partly you can, and partly you can't, I suppose. Well, about fightin': it ain't likely 'twill ever come your turn to do that; leastwise, we don't calculate on havin' a war in your day."

"If there is one, I'll go and fight, grandfather; I promise you that!"

"Why, I hope so, boy,—that is, if it's a war to uphold the right and presarve the libbaties of your country. War is a dreadful thing, and I hope it may never come to this happy land; but, if it does, I hope nobody who's got a single drop of my blood in their veins will suffer that old flag to be dishonoured."

Leonard placed his hand silently on his grandfather's knee, in token that he never would.

"I hope you'll never have to fight, my boy; but there is one thing you will have to do if you live, and that is, to vote."

"Yes, I know that: everybody has to vote in town-meeting once a year."

"Yes, each citizen has to vote in town-meetin', and in that way he governs the country, or, rather, helps to make the laws which govern the country. This is the way it's done. You go to town-meetin' here in Woodlee, and you vote for men to go to the State Legislature and to Congress; and these men, when they get there, make laws for the State and nation. So, you see, if you go and vote for John Pease, and John Pease is a bad man, who don't care nothin' about his country, but only jist how to git into office and sarve his own ends, then you've done your country an injury; mabbe not a dreadful sight at first, but you've done it some; for if John Pease is a bad man he'll be pretty likely to do all he can to make bad laws, and you are to blame for the bad laws he makes: don't you see?"

"Yes, grandfather; but then we are governed by a President."

"No, we ain't, my boy; we are governed by laws, and the President don't make these laws: he only sees they're put in force, or executed: so that he is sometimes called the *Executive*. Really, the President don't have but dreadful little power in ordinary times. He can't make a single law: only if he's a mind to stop a law he can. It ain't a law till he's signed his name to it; and if he don't choose to do that, he ain't obliged to: he may decline, and give his reasons for it. This is what is called using his *veto*. But when a law has passed thro' Congress and he has signed it, so that it is really a law of the nation, he must see it is carried out, or executed.

And in a time of war, he stands at the head of all our armies, is 'Commander-in-chief of the army and navy of the United States:' that's what the Constitution says."

"But who makes the President, grandfather?"

"Why, the people,—everybody who votes. They choose in town-meetin' men called electors, and these electors say who shall be the next President. If I want Jackson to be our President, I vote for the electors who'll put him in; and if I want Clay to be the President, I vote for the men who'll put him in. So, you see, I do as much as any other man towards makin' our President; for one vote counts just as much as another. The poorest man in Woodlee puts in one vote, and the Governor himself can't put in any more. We are all on the same footing in this matter of voting. Folks ain't on the same footing in every thing. Some folks are richer than others, and some are handsomer and stronger and smarter, and always will be; but the rich man does no more to make laws for us than the poor man: them's the equal rights folks have in this country, and they don't have 'em in any other that ever I've heerd on. Now, if folks ain't good themselves, they won't vote for good men: so the very first thing towards bein' a patriot is to be a good man yourself."

"Yes," added the old gentleman, after a little pause, "every man in this country has got to vote, and he's got to larn how to vote."

"Learn how? I don't understand that," said Leonard.

"Why, he's got to get eddication enough to understand about things, and how they ought to be done in the country. Then he'll know a good law from a poor one, and how to send men to the Legislatur' that will make the right sort of ones. You'll be a voter, Leonard, when you are twenty-one; and afore that time comes, it's your solemn duty to larn how to vote in such a way that your country will be the better for your voting. You must go to school and learn about the different countries in the world, and their kind of government, and about the history and government of your own country: so that you can tell what's good for the country and what ain't. Eddication, every citizen of a free country must have; and he must have somethin' else, too: he must have piety,—that is, the love and fear of God in his heart. If a man loves God, he will love justice and libbaty, and will want justice and libbaty to prevail in the land. Allers remember, Leonard, that it takes two things to make a good voter and a good patriot,—for the two are pretty much the same thing, I take it, in our country,— and these are *knowledge and piety*. Remember this as long as you live; and never forget that the man who votes understandingly, and in the fear of God, is the man who loves his country and is doing what he can to have her well governed and prosperous."

"But there are some people, grandfather, who can't get much education: how will they learn how to vote?"

"It's true all men can't have a sight of book-larnin', for they don't get time to study; but, thank God, there ain't no man in this country who can't get knowledge enough to understand something about the laws and government of the land, and about her history; and if he don't, it's his own fault, for we've got schools for every child. If he's born in a poor-house, it don't make any difference: he can go to school till he's sixteen without its costin' him a single cent. So, if our voters don't know enough to discarn between right and wrong, it's their own fault. But they do know, and can tell the difference. Bless me! don't they talk politics by the hour in every bar-room, and store, and shoemaker's-shop, the country over; and if they don't allers talk sound doctrine, 'tain't because they don't know enough: it's because they ain't good enough: that's the trouble! They don't want to see the right upheld and justice prosper!"

The old man stopped and sighed heavily, and turned his cane round and round, as if some painful thought had risen in his mind.

"Yes, folks ain't good enough: that's the trouble! They ain't honest enough: they don't love God enough. If they loved God, they'd love right and justice, and want to see 'em done to every human bein'. If ever trouble comes, it won't be because we are ignorant, so long as we have a schoolhouse on every hill and in every valley: it will be because we are dishonest, and corrupt, and love wickedness, and have forgot God and his commandments: that's what I'm afeard on!" And he sighed again.

"But some have to learn how to be representatives, and Governors, and other great men, grandfather."

"Don't talk o' that, Leonard! Office-holdin' ain't what belongs to folks in general; and if it did, the way to be a good officer is to be a good citizen,—to stay at home and mind your own business. The man who runs around to get himself into notice, and thinks he's fittin' himself for some great things, is jist the man who ain't fit for nothin': he's only puffed up, jist like a bladder, with nothin' in't but wind. Why, how do you think George Washington made himself fit for a gineral and a President? By just bein' a steady, likely boy, who went to school regular, and allers told the truth, and got his lessons, and minded his father and mother. The seeds was planted in him, the seeds of honesty and patriotism, while he was quietly doin' his duty every day, like any other good boy; and when he got to be a man, they sprouted up and bore fruit to the blessin' and savin' of his country. Do you suppose if he'd a lied, or cheated, or been lazy, he'd a made such a gineral as he did? No, indeed: pretty likely he'd a been like Benedict Arnold, that old traitor, who allers lied!

Do you jist go to school, Leonard, and larn all you can, and mind your parents, and tell the truth, and do what is right; and then, if God's gin you any great abilities, they'll show themselves fast enough; and if he's called you to do any great work for your country, never fear but that you'll do it in his own good time. But don't go to thinkin' about bein' fit for office. That's just the worst thing a boy or man can do. There's allers men enough to make the laws. You do your best to obey them. Law is all we have to govern us in our country; and a true patriot is the man who votes as he ought to, and obeys the laws of his country as well as he knows how."

"What if it's a bad law? Must he obey then?"

"Yes, till it is changed. The way to mend that in our country is to get the bad law altered,—not to despise it while it is a law of the land. As long as we send good men to make the laws, the laws will be good. Make it a matter of conscience, my boy, to obey the laws, for this is the only way that a free people like us can hev any rights; and he who disobeys the law cannot be a good citizen. I am afraid we don't think of this enough. It's the main pillar that our freedom and prosperity rest on, and all that keeps us from goin'· to destruction."

The old gentleman had evidently forgotten the presence of his youthful auditor, and sat with bowed head, as if some vision of the future rose darkly before him. If so, it passed away; for he raised his face in a moment and looked upward with cheerful trust.

"The God of our fathers," he said, reverently, "who brought them over the wide ocean and set them in a large place, and has made of us a great people,—the mighty God of Jacob, he can presarve us still, and cause us to love and serve him through all comin' generations."

"Be a true patriot, Leonard?" he added,

after a few moments' silence. "Yes, indeed you can be! You can love God and fear him, and pray to him night and day, as long as you live, to save your country from ignorance and sin. You can be an honest man yourself; you can try to make other men honest; and you can do all that in you lies to put honest, God-fearing men into office. Yes, you can be a patriot, my boy: God grant you allers may be one!"

The setting sun threw its last beams on the bared head of the old sea-captain, and rested on his gray hairs like a crown of glory. Leonard felt a new love and veneration for him; and, as he sat at the door of that lonely cottage among the hills, a desire to be truthful and honest and good sprang up in the heart of the boy, and, though unuttered, something like a resolve that, God helping him, he would become a true patriot, stirred in the depths of his boyish soul.

## CHAPTER V.

### A DAY IN SCHOOL.

There can be no doubt that such conversations as these had an influence on Leonard, though at the time he thought little about them. Boys of his age do not think much. It is a receptive age, when they see and hear and feel, but do not shape their mental processes into definite ideas. What is thus received, however, is the material out of which the man is made; for always, silently, hour by hour, the boy is becoming moulded into the future man, and every surrounding influence has its share in determining what the character of that man shall be.

The stories his grandfather liked to tell him about his battles, and his repeated injunctions to be always upright and honest and true to the flag, all had their influence on Leonard; but far more powerful was the daily life he saw lived in the red house. It was a life of continued toil and self-denial in order that their debts might be paid; and it taught lessons every hour. Parents who live on borrowed means, who resort to all kinds of tricks and deceptions to get rid of paying their honest debts,— they too teach lessons to their children; and how is it possible that such can grow into upright, honourable men and women?

Never would Mary Roberts's children forget the look of astonishment and rebuke which she one day cast on the lawyer who advised her not to sign the deed of mortgage, thereby retaining her right to dower.

"Not do all I can to pay my husband's debts?" she said, looking up into his face with her straightforward eyes. "I would rather die in the poor-house an honest woman, than live in luxury with our debts unpaid!"

"But this is a hard case," said the lawyer, who had come from a neighbouring town to assist in arranging matters, and meant kindly by the suggestion. "If your husband had had the benefit of the money, it would have been different; but, being only an endorser, there was really no value received."

"He became responsible for the debt by his own free act," replied the wife, quietly. "It was a very unwise thing, as it proved; but the creditor is entitled to his money just the same: it is not his fault that the principal failed, or that my husband signed the note. No, it is an honest debt, and it shall be honestly paid, God giving us health and strength!"

Probably the attorney still thought her over-scrupulous, and possibly she was; but, if every wife and mother in our land would teach such lessons as these, we should soon hear little of swindling contractors, knavish law-officers, or fraudulent merchants and mechanics. The want of an *honest* home-training,—is it not the great want of our time and nation? Fathers, mothers, are you by your daily life teaching your children to be honest,— to pay their debts at whatever sacrifice, and never to take or keep what is not justly their's?

The next day, as Leonard and Sydney went past Mr. Hall's, who lived at the foot of the long hill, John Hall was waiting for them at the gate; and by the time they reached the turn in the road, there were Susan and Sarah Lee coming from the opposite direction. So the five children went on together. After turning, their road lay through a piece of uncleared woods.

"I say, let's have some fun out of Nat Rowe," said John: "he's got a parcel of butternuts hid up here somewhere. I guess they're around this hollow tree. He's calculating to have a great crack one of these days; but we'll hide 'em; and won't he look astonished when he finds they are all gone?"

Leonard was ready enough for fun. Besides, Nat Rowe was what all the boys called stingy, and no favourite at best.

"But where shall we carry them?" he asked.

"Oh, we'll throw 'em into the brook; he won't be likely to find them there, I reckon."

"But it will be wicked to waste them," said Susan Lee: "butternuts are so good."

"I don't care for that," said John, "if we can only put 'em where he won't see 'em again."

After a long search, the nuts were discovered in a little hollow place, surrounded by loose stones and covered over with leaves.

"There ain't so very many, after all," said John. "Suppose we just divide 'em among ourselves. I can carry my share in my pocket, and here are the girls' bags, —a capital place to put 'em in."

"I don't want the dirty things in *my*

bag," said little Sarah, in a doleful voice: "they'll spoil my patchwork."

"Then throw 'em into the brook and done with it!" said John. And the younger children began to gather them up gleefully for that purpose.

"No, we won't put them in the brook," said Leonard. "They don't belong to us. They're Nat's; and, if he *is* a mean, stingy fellow, we haven't any right to take his things. I don't mind hiding them for fun; by-and-by we can tell him where they are, or carry them back; but I won't throw them in the brook."

"Bosh! I don't believe in being so notional," exclaimed John, pettishly. "I guess he'll find 'em: if he can't, he won't starve."

"They belong to him," said Leonard, more decidedly. "He took ever so much pains to pick them up, and we haven't any right to *his* things."

"Then you haven't any right to move 'em at all," said John: "*we haven't any right to his things,*" he added, drawling out the words in an absurd imitation of Leonard's tone, which made all the others laugh.

Leonard's fist instantly closed with a boy's instinct to show fight; but he changed his mind, and said, rather crossly, "No, we haven't; and I won't have any thing to do with it! It's time we were going to school."

"So 'tis," said Susan Lee. "I don't want a tardy-mark." So they set off, John and Leonard both a little disturbed in spirit.

"I suppose you expect to get the medal to-night," said Susan, playfully, to Leonard; "but you won't. I've studied my lesson over ten times, and I sha'n't miss a word. But, if I do get down, I'd rather you would be at the head than anybody else."

"I'll bet I can beat you both," cried John. "What if I am at the head myself, Miss Lee?"

Susan laughed merrily. "Oh, you won't

be. You're away down at the foot,—all but one,—you know."

"But I can study if I've a mind to."

They all knew he could; but he was such an idle, careless fellow, he seldom tried to do his best.

They soon left the woods, and came out on the little level grass-plot on which the school-house stood, and where some twenty or thirty children were now gathered. A moment after, the bell rang, and they all went in,—the girls hanging their bonnets on a row of nails upon one side of the entry, and the boys their caps on another row opposite.

The exercises of the school went on as usual. First a chapter from the Bible was read, then a short prayer, after which each class read in turn, beginning with the oldest, and ending with the little ones who sat on the small bench and were worrying through the mysteries of "b-a–ba, b-e–be."

Susan, John and Leonard belonged to the third class. Miss Brace had promised a present to the pupil in each class who should have the greatest number of marks for perfect lessons at the close of the term. The members of the third class were so nearly on a level in capacity and attainments that there was a keen strife among them to win this prize. Whoever was at the head went to the foot at the close of the day, to work his way up again as best he could; and whoever was at the head wore home the medal,—a silver dollar with a hole in it, through which a bright-coloured ribbon was passed; and supremely happy was the child who wore that medal home. In addition, a prize was to be given to whoever during the term should have gained the most tickets for good behaviour,— a ticket being given only when there had been some unusual excellence in conduct. Delighted as they all were to get the medal, the tiny bits of pasteboard with "*Good Behaviour*" written on them were still more coveted, perhaps because so much more rarely obtained.

This day, Martha James stood at the head of the third class, Susan Lee next, and, below her, Leonard Roberts: so that any failure on Susan's part would bring Leonard to the head at night,—the place which Susan would have if she was perfect in all her lessons. Both Susan and Leonard studied their lessons very diligently after they had finished reading; for the third class was the first to spell after recess. For a wonder, John Hall was also quite industriously studying his: so that Miss Brace was not obliged to keep her eye perpetually on his corner; and she was careful to give him a word of commendation as she passed by him. "If John would only really apply himself," she said, as if to herself, "he might make such a fine scholar,—he's so bright and quick-witted."

After recess, the boys came rushing in, hot and breathless from their sports; and only a brief space was given them to compose themselves, when the words, "Third class, take your places," rang through the room. Out they marched in obedience to the summons,—No. 1, No. 2, No. 3, and so on to the last, No. 8,—all ranging themselves by a crack in the floor. The majority had bare feet; but who cared for that? It was heads, not feet, that were to be thought of then,—only as each looked down to be sure his were exactly on the crack. Their bright faces showed they were all confident of acquitting themselves well; and John Hall, though down at No. 7, looked as complacent as any of them. As it happened, Clara Jones missed a word the first time round, which brought him up to No. 6. John certainly was fortunate that day; for both No. 4 and No. 5 afterwards missed a word, which was quite an unusual thing; and, having studied his lesson thoroughly, John, for a wonder, could spell it rightly, and with a triumphant toss of his curly head he walked up and placed himself next to Leonard Roberts, into whose side he gave a most significant nudge, that he might be fully aware of the fact. Perhaps this success stimulated John to new efforts; for he had but one failure in his arithmetic-lesson,—a most remarkable event. So at the close of the morning session our three friends were in excellent spirits.

In the afternoon, the classes went through the same rouitne of reading and spelling. The excitement in the third class was greater, because if Susan Lee failed now she lost the medal. But she was known to be a good scholar, and no one expected she would fail: so the chief interest was in watching Leonard, who would be the medal-boy the next day if he kept his place,— which was by no means sure, as he often missed a word.

The second time round, Clara Jones missed another word, and went down again, with a flood of tears; but she was so near the foot that her change of place was of no vital importance. At the fourth and last round, the word *achievement* came to Leonard, who spelt it promptly, a-ch *c i* v e—

ment, ment,—achievement. "Try again, Leonard," said Miss Brace. There was a profound stillness in the school-room. Not only that class, but all the others, looked up and listened. The question of *ins* and *outs* was quite as interesting to them as in the political circles to which they might one day belong.

Perhaps the consciousness that so much was at stake confused Leonard; for, though he had studied his lesson so thoroughly that he felt sure when he came out he could spell every word, he now hesitated and was at a loss. Miss Brace's back was turned an instant, and Susan Lee whispered "*ie*," very softly; but Leonard heard it, and the second time spelled it "a-c h i e v e-m e n t."

"Right," said Miss Brace; and the spelling went on quietly.

But all was not quiet in Leonard's bosom. A strong feeling of shame at his deception was rankling there. He was keeping his place, not because he was entitled to it, but on false pretences; and his face grew very red from this inward conflict; but no one was looking at him.

Martha James went to the foot, resigning her medal to Miss Brace as she passed down. Susan Lee took her place at the head of the class, and Miss Brace was placing the medal, with a smile, round her neck, when she was startled by a half-sob which came from Leonard.

"I should have missed if she hadn't told me!" he exclaimed, in an excited tone, making a great effort to suppress his emotion. There had been a struggle. He was sorely tempted to let the deception pass unnoticed, and retain his place; but the principle of honour and justice had triumphed. He would not keep his place by acting a lie.

"It is against the rules to tell," said Miss Brace, with a cloud on her face. "It is a wrong thing to do; and I am very sorry to find any one in the class has been guilty of it. It is in effect a falsehood to pretend to know a word when you do not. I am very glad, Leonard, that you are too honourable to take advantage of such a deception, and I hope you will always be too upright to keep a place in your class, or anywhere else, which does not rightfully belong to you."

Then came the question whether John should go up. It was a difficult one to settle, for it was not sure he would have been able to spell the word,—though he probably would, as he had studied so diligently that day. The school-room was hushed to hear the decision.

"I want to have exact justice done," said Miss Brace, "but it is very difficult to tell what justice does require in this case. It is clear that Leonard ought to lose his place, as he could not spell the word; but it is not so clear that John ought to take it."

"I am willing he should," said Leonard, whose face had now cleared, and was beaming with the consciousness of having acted rightly. "I ought to go down, and I almost know John would have spelt it right."

John's moral sense was not very acute, usually; but there is something contagious in a right action. Leonard's honest avowal had affected every scholar in the class, and each of them was now more likely to do right in consequence of it. So John said, very modestly,—

"I think I could have spelt it, but I don't care about going up. May-be I should have missed it."

But Leonard had already moved to exchange places with him, and Miss Brace allowed the exchange to be made.

"I am a little doubtful of the propriety of it," she said; "but one thing is certain: Leonard is much happier in being No. 3 with a clear conscience, than No. 2 with a guilty one; and John deserves some reward for his unusual industry. He has studied so faithfully to-day he ought to be able to spell every word correctly."

Leonard and John both looked a little shy, as some boys are apt to do when praised, but both went to their seats with beaming faces. When the time came for distributing the tickets (always an event of great interest), Miss Brace held them a moment in her hand, and said,—

"I take particular pleasure to-night in giving one of you a ticket for good behaviour, because he has shown himself too honest to deceive me when he might have done it without being detected."

She then called on Leonard to come forward, who did so, and received the ticket with a deep blush, while all the school gazed at him with admiring eyes and wished themselves in his place. Miss Brace glanced at the earnest faces on the seats before her, and added, with much emotion,—

"How I wish I could impress one lesson upon all my pupils, and impress it so strongly that you could never forget it! and that is, *never to act on false pretences;*

*never to deceive in any way.* Children are apt to think that to deceive by their actions is not so bad as to tell a direct lie; but the sin is the same in God's sight. The guilt of lying consists in the deception practised; and if you deceive others by keeping silent, it is just as wrong as to deceive them by speaking falsely. I want you all to abhor what is false in every shape,—false words, false acts, false looks.

"Oh, if all of you would grow up into truthful, honest men and women," she added, with her cheek glowing and her eye beaming, "and go out into the world too high-minded ever to equivocate, or ever to occupy false positions, or ever to keep what does not rightfully belong to you, what noble men and women you would make! You would then be blessings to the world, and such men and women as all good beings would honour and God himself approve!"

Susan Lee was desired to remain, as Miss Brace wished to impress on her mind more clearly the evils of prompting, and in that way tempting another scholar to act a falsehood.

Had any one told Leonard Roberts in the morning that when he came over that road at night John Hall would be above him in his class, and that instead of being miserable about it he would feel more light-hearted than usual, he would have said it was impossible: yet so it was. With that little ticket buttoned into his jacket-pocket, to be shown to his mother and grandfather, and that consciousness of having done right lying warm at his heart, he was a happy boy; and neither he nor John once thought of the butternuts when they went by the place.

"I say, ain't Miss Brace prime?" exclaimed John. "When a fellow tries to do, she always knows it. But I did feel kind of mean going up above you; that's a fact!"

"You needn't," answered Leonard, cheerily. "I don't feel one bit bad about it, and I hope you'll get the medal,—I do really, John; though I tell you I mean to study as hard as I can, so that if you miss I can just step into your place. That's fair!"

"So 'tis!" said John; and they parted the best of friends.

Did Leonard remember that he had taken one step that day towards becoming a true patriot? Probably not; but it was none the less true that he had.

## CHAPTER VI.

### THE FISHING-PARTY.

JOHN HALL kept his place through the next day, and at night had the satisfaction of wearing home the medal. It *was* a satisfaction, though he pretended to care nothing about it, and even tucked it out of sight on the way home, saying, " He couldn't be bothered with having that thing right in his way all the time." John was a peculiar boy, with an odd mixture of shyness and boldness, pride and sensitiveness, in his composition; and he was very ambitious, withal, in a certain way.

As they were going home, he laid before Leonard a magnificent plan for the next Saturday afternoon. This was nothing less than a *trout-fry*. Three boys, two of them cousins of his, were coming over from a neighbouring town to spend the day. They were older than himself, and wished to fish in the streams of Woodlee; and John proposed to ask Leonard and Nathan Joy to accompany them, and to have a grand frolic. A trout-fry answers to a clam-bake, only changing the clams to trout,—the sandy beach, with its dashing salt waves, to a green meadow with a rippling brook running through it,—and the baking to frying. There is the same fresh, out-of-door enjoyment and abandonment to the pleasure of the moment in both, the same keen appetite, and the same mirth-provoking deficiency of cooking and table utensils of all kinds.

The boys of Woodlee were all accustomed to fishing; for a clear trout-stream ran about among its hills, called the Brook, or sometimes Willow Brook, probably because there were some dwarf-willows overhanging it just below the village. But they had always brought their fish home in a string, to be cooked by their mothers; for a trout-fry was an enjoyment indulged in only by grown pleasure-seekers, and seldom by them, unless when visitors came to the place, in whose honour little fishing-parties were sometimes made up.

The more John and Leonard talked over the project, the more feasible and delightful it looked to them. There was one drawback,—a doubt whether Leonard's father would consent to his going. On Saturday afternoons, the only half-holiday then given in schools, Leonard frequently went to mill; and he expected to be obliged to go the coming Saturday. He usually liked this, for it gave him a ride of three miles in which he drove himself. He liked to drive; and he liked also to saunter round the mill, watching the grain as it went into the hopper, or the water pouring over the dam, or, as sometimes happened, having conversation with the miller and his sons, who always helped him to unload, and, when his grist was ground, to load up again, and who on such occasions often praised him as "a smart young fellow who could give a stout lift." But, pleasant as all this was in ordinary times, it was nothing to a trout-fry.

"Can't you put it off one Saturday?" he asked, eagerly. "Next week I sha'n't have to go to mill."

"No, because Tom and Harry won't be here again all summer. They're coming over on purpose to go a fishing."

"I almost know I shall have to go to mill; everybody else is busy, and I heard father say to-day the meal was just gone."

"I'm glad I don't have to work so hard as you do," said John: "you are always doing chores till dark, and you never get any time for fun."

"I know it," said Leonard, dolefully, "I wish we weren't so poor; but we are: so there's no help for it!"

"Well, I hope something will turn up so you can go Saturday. We shall have a splendid time. Mother says we may carry the large spider, and have as much pork as we want, and a pie or two besides. Yes, we shall have a first-rate time, I'm sure of that!"

Leonard sighed again; and, after parting with John, he walked on slowly, thinking of the hardships of his lot. Yes, he always did have to work. After he got home from school, there was weeding in the garden, and errands to be done; then he must go to the pasture for the cows; then milk, and split up kindlings, and bring in wood and water. John Hall could go down to the Centre every night and play ball with the down-town boys, while he had to run his feet off for everybody. The more he thought of it, the harder his lot seemed, and the more he pitied himself on account of it; and he exclaimed,—

"I wonder why some folks always have to work like slaves all their lives long, while others grow up gentlemen and never have to lift a finger?"

It is an old question, Leonard,—one asked centuries ago, and which has been repeated by every generation since, and yet is no nearer being solved. So you need not vex your brain with it, but, like a stout, brave-hearted boy as you are, just learn to submit to what is inevitable, and get all the enjoyment you can out of the life God has given you,—a life which you may make a rich and noble one in spite of all its hardships, if you do not get a habit of grumbling over them.

"I wonder," he continued to himself, "what we need to be so in debt for? I never can have any thing I want, nor father nor mother either, because *that* debt must be paid!"

Yet the thought of his parents labouring on so patiently, day after day, softened his feelings, and he could not feel sorry that he was able to do a little something to help them.

Ah, if the boy who was walking along that shaded road that night with bare feet and stout, vigorous frame could only have had the veil lifted, and looked on life as perhaps the watching angels view it from their serene abodes, would he not have seen that this very habit of daily toil was a blessed safeguard from a thousand sorer evils? Would he not have found that this very necessity of exerting himself for others was making him more manly, more like Him who came not to be ministered unto, but to minister? But of course he could not see this; for many things are hidden from the eyes of both boys and men.

Arrived at home, Leonard told his mother of John's delightful plans, and of his wishes and fears. It was then only Wednesday:—did she think he could go?

"I wish you could, with all my heart," she answered, "but I am afraid the men will all be too busy to go to mill: so that if the meal is wanted you will have to go for it. You must do all you can to help along, you know, Leonard."

"But it's hard I can't ever have a play-day!"

"A great many things in this life are hard," said his mother; and, with this not very consoling reflection, she sent him out to split up kindlings to boil the tea-kettle.

Mary Roberts could usually see the silver lining to each cloud; but that night she was very tired, and not in a hopeful mood herself. Poor woman! She wanted her children to enjoy themselves, and often sighed to think they had so few opportunities.

"Can't I drive over to the mill, mother?" asked Mabel. "The white-faced horse is pretty steady."

"*You!*" exclaimed Lucy. "You'd look grandly, driving a load of bags through the street!"

"I don't care for the looks," said Mabel; "that is, not much; and I do care a great deal to have Leonard go. He never goes berrying, or fishing, or any thing else, as the other boys do; and he's such a dear, good boy, and so willing to do all we want him to do! I sha'n't mind the looks: the bags will be in the bottom of the wagon, and the men at the mill will unload them for me."

"I hardly think your father will be willing you should drive over," said her mother. "He won't think it's of much consequence whether Leonard goes or not."

"I think father is a great deal too strict with Leonard," said Lucy. "He never lets him go from home, not even to play ball with the other boys."

Mrs. Roberts herself thought her husband erred on the side of strictness; but it did not suit her ideas of propriety to have her youngest daughter pertly criticizing his mode of government.

"He does what he thinks is best for Leonard," she answered; "he doesn't like to have him playing with all kinds of boys, and there are some down town from whom he wouldn't learn any thing good."

"Yes," said Mabel, "there's Nat Rowe

and Jim Baker are dreadfully profane. I shouldn't want him to go with them."

"He is so fond of a book when he gets time to sit down," said his mother, "that he isn't lonesome. Then, too, he likes to hear grandfather's stories about the sea; and Sydney is a great deal of company for him. After all," she added, her face brightening, "I dare say he enjoys himself as well as most boys; and he's learning lessons that will be of use to him all his life. It isn't the boys that are always indulged and know nothing about hardships that make the finest men." Mabel was ready to acknowledge this.

"The very necessity for making sacrifices," continued the mother, "brings a certain kind of pleasure with it. You are happier this moment, Mabel, because you are willing to lay aside a bit of foolish pride for Leonard's sake."

"Yes, I am always happier when I give up any thing for him, or you either, dear mother. I wish I could learn to be always unselfish."

"You are learning it constantly, my dear girl, and are more and more a comfort to me every day of your life. Our life seems a hard one," she said, after a little pause, "yet it has a good deal of brightness in it: sometimes I think those who can have all they want without any trouble, lose a good deal of enjoyment. How much satisfaction we take in planning how to bring things round just right, saving here and contriving there, so as to secure some pleasure we couldn't otherwise enjoy! Yes, I really believe we are happier even for our self-denials, and for having to make sacrifices for one another."

"I suppose we are; but it doesn't seem at all pleasant at the time," said Mabel.

"'No affliction for the time seemeth joyous, but grievous.' It wouldn't be a sacrifice if it didn't cost something; and just in proportion to the pain is the pleasure that comes after."

"*I* don't like to give up," said Lucy. "If I have to, I do; but I don't enjoy doing it, first or last."

A little sigh escaped from the mother's heart. She was afraid it was really so, and that her youngest and fairest daughter had never yet learned the delight of voluntarily relinquishing her own ease or enjoyment for the sake of others.

"If you do it because you must, of course there is no pleasure in it," she said. "It is in choosing to make a sacrifice for another that we find a higher joy than in possession."

When Mr. Roberts had finished his day's work, and sat by his back door resting himself, his wife spoke to him about Leonard's plans and wishes, and of Mabel's offer to go to mill in his place. As she had expected, he rejected the latter proposal at once.

"Send a girl to mill, indeed! that would be a strange way of doing things. I'd quite as soon Leonard should keep away from all such parties. There's no good in boys running round all the time. Leonard has got to work for a living; and the sooner he learns to attend to business and let other things alone, the better."

He evidently had no faith in the proverb that "All work and no play makes Jack a dull boy." Mrs. Roberts sighed, but she knew her husband too well to attempt to argue the subject with him. So, saying to herself, "It is only Wednesday, and before Saturday something may happen to change his mind," she went out and strained the foaming pails of milk which had just been brought into the sweet, clean pantry.

## CHAPTER VII.

### THE DECISION.

'Good news!" shouted John Hall, when he saw Leonard coming down the hill the next morning. "The water has broken through the dam, so they can't grind there for a week or more. Aren't you glad?"

" Yes, indeed," cried Leonard, throwing his hat up into the air, exultingly; " now I can go fishing Saturday. *Hurrah!*"

It seemed like a special interposition of Providence in his behalf, and he did not trouble himself to remember that it might bring great inconvenience to others. No lad accustomed to holiday excursions can have any idea how desirable and delightful this little pleasure-party looked to Leonard. If he had few pleasures, they were all the brighter when they came; and the prospect of this one made all study easier to him that day, and all play merrier.

Leonard kept his place; and so he wore the medal home proudly and joyfully. He was indeed a happy boy that night! His mother and Mabel sympathized with his joy and his hopes,—though the former said she was afraid it would be inconvenient to many families to have the mill stopped, and prove a great loss to the miller himself. But Leonard only thought of the pleasure in store for him the next Saturday. His usually cool head was quite turned by it, and he teased his mother by perpetually questioning her about the weather, and what he might carry for his share of the great entertainment.

Friday night at last came. "It will be cloudy to-morrow, I guess, and so much the better," said Leonard to John, as they came home from school: "the trout will bite all the sharper. We'll go first to Burnall's pond. Nobody has fished there lately, and there'll be lots of trout there; and we can cook them in the old woods."

"Old woods" was the name given to a beautiful strip of forest which skirted the pond, where the trees had stood untouched for a century; and it was the most delightful place imaginable for a picnic, with its deep shade and soft carpet of matted leaves.

Just at this point, Susan Lee rushed up in breathless haste, exclaiming, "The mill is running again. Do you hear, Leonard?"

"No, I don't believe a word of it," he answered, indignantly. "Sawyer said it would take ten days to start it."

"But it is," persisted Susan. "I heard Deacon Harris say so just now. He called out to Roswell Pease and told him, and said he was going to carry over some grain to-night."

But Leonard had too strong reasons for not believing, to credit any such testimony. "It's just a girl's story," he said, contemptuously. "Why, John, it can't be running yet?"

"I guess not," said John, evasively. The truth was, he had heard in the morning that the mill was running, but he chose to keep Leonard in ignorance of the fact.

A little farther on, they met Sawyer, one of the workmen at the mill, coming towards them in a wagon. He would know the true state of things there.

"The mill isn't running yet, Mr. Sawyer, is it?" asked Leonard, anxiously.

"Yes, we got it a-going again last night. The foundation wasn't washed away: so we stopped up the hole a good deal quicker than we expected." And he rode along as if he had conveyed the most pleasant piece of intelligence. Leonard was confounded: he felt as if a great stone had fallen on his heart, crushing out all its hopes.

"I hope you'll believe the next time you hear a girl's story," was Susan Lee's parting observation, as she turned into the path that led towards her home.

"It's too bad!" said Leonard. "Now I shall have to go to mill to-morrow. I know I shall; for father said this morning he didn't see how he could get along without having some grinding done. I never can have any fun!" he added, bitterly.

"It's a shame, I declare!" said John. "I wouldn't go an inch, let who would tell me to."

Leonard had been too well trained to habits of obedience to think of opposing his father's commands, but he felt bitterly injured.

"I'll tell you what 'tis," said John, consolingly: "your father won't know the mill is going. He's been working all the morning among his hay, and hasn't seen anybody to tell him, I know. Do you just keep whist, and he'll never be the wiser."

"I don't think he's heard of it," said Leonard. It was a pleasant idea; but, after a moment's satisfaction in it, he said, "But I don't think it will be quite fair not to tell him, John."

"Why, what a fuss you always make about being fair! What's the harm, I should like to know? If 'twas telling a lie, it would be a different thing; but holding your tongue can't be a sin, I'm sure."

"Perhaps it isn't," said Leonard, for he wanted to think there wasn't any harm in it. So they went on planning about the excursion the same as before; and John's last words were, "Be sure and bring plenty of bait, and all your hooks."

If there was a question in Leonard's mind of the propriety of concealing the fact from his father, he put it down by thinking he couldn't fall back from the party now. He had said he would go, and he must go.

"How lucky it is Sydney didn't come to school to-day!" thought he, as he walked on. "He would have been sure to tell."

Leonard didn't feel quite easy in his mind, for he was afraid somebody might have given the information; but he soon found by the conversation of his mother and sisters that they were still in ignorance, and congratulated himself greatly on the fact.

Why was it that Leonard did not go about his work that night with quite so light a heart as usual,—that his bread-and-milk had a less keen relish,—that he started when anybody spoke suddenly, as if afraid he was going to be exposed? Leonard's nature and training had made it far easier for him to be frank than to conceal a thing; and his secret hung like a heavy weight on his spirits. If it had been any common sacrifice demanded of him, he would have made it; but to give up this pleasure, so long looked forward to and coveted, and which he probably would never have another chance to enjoy, —it was too much; and over and over again he said to himself, as he split up his kindlings, "There can't be any harm in just keeping still. I don't tell any falsehood."

Boys accustomed to evasions and concealments might never have thought of any harm in one of this kind; but in the atmosphere of the red house, and in the light of his mother's example, Leonard's conscience had become very tender, and averse to any thing not thoroughly open and upright.

After tea, Leonard went for his cows, as usual. The pasture was half a mile distant, and the way to it was through a wood in which there was only a narrow path trodden by the cows. As he walked through this dense pine woods, Leonard became thoughtful. It seemed as if a voice spoke to him, saying, "You are deceiving, Leonard; you know you are!" Whence could that voice have come? From those dark pines which shot up so tall and straight towards the sky? No: they were perfectly motionless; and though a soft, sweet, spirit-like whisper stole through their branches, it was not that he heard. From the shining heavens above him? No: there were bright patches of soft blue visible far away beyond the pines, and they looked smilingly down at him, but it was not they who spoke. From the little brook, which went trickling on its way like a thread of silver, gurgling over the mossy stones, and then dipping with a musical tinkle into the grassy hollow? No: its song was most wonderful and sweet, but it was not that he heard. It was a voice in his own breast,—the voice of conscience, —the voice of God! It startled him at first, and, when he attempted to silence it by saying he was telling no falsehood, he heard it sounding clearer yet, and uttering Miss Brace's very words, "The guilt of lying is in the deception used; and if you deceive by keeping silent, it is just as wrong as if you deceived by speaking falsely." Leonard felt indignant. He would not be kept from his enjoyment to-morrow; that he was determined on; right or wrong, he would go to that fishing-party! and he trod fiercely on the withered leaves. Then he caught up a stone and aimed it at a harmless little squirrel that was skipping up a tree. As it happened, it did not hurt the pretty, bright-eyed creature; but it was no thanks to him. But all did not silence the voice within. Its tones rose up strong and distinct above all other sounds. "You are deceiving," it said, sternly; "you are gaining a selfish gratification under false pretences!"

The true nature of his conduct was thus clearly revealed to Leonard: it now remained for him to decide whether he would persist in it. He must now fight one of those battles so often fought in human hearts,—a battle between inclination and duty, between right and wrong. Silent, unheard-of conflicts are these, but often as fierce and desperate as if waged by armed men at the cannon's mouth.

His desire to go was strong, passionately strong, and it pleaded stoutly for the victory; but, on the other hand, con-

"He caught up a stone and aimed it at a harmless little squirrel that was skipping up a tree."   p. 100.

science also contended manfully for the right. To deceive was mean; to obtain a pleasure through false pretences was cowardly and unmanly. To go home and tell his father that the mill was running, and abide the consequences, was a straightforward, upright course; not to tell him, was to play a false part and to deceive intentionally. Which should he do?

It was a hard struggle in the boy's heart; and it was far from being ended when he emerged from the wood into the open ground. It was a broken, stony region, and he sat down on a huge flat rock to decide the question. It was not Leonard's way to flinch from trouble, or to put off what was disagreeable: he always faced the worst, and had things settled as soon as possible.

"This is a very little thing," you may say: "nothing is at stake but a schoolboy's half-day frolic. It is of no particular consequence whether he goes or stays." But it was of consequence,—not the thing itself, but the principle involved. A series of such decisions as these by the boy make the habits of the man,—habits which, once fixed, it is wellnigh impossible to overcome. If Leonard now yield to this temptation to deviate from a strictly straightforward course, he may become a man of shifts and artifices and concealments; if he overcome it, his moral nature will be strengthened, and he will be far more likely to make a thoroughly honest, upright, truthful man. So it may be that as the boy sits there in his patched, homespun clothes, a torn straw hat on his head, and his bare feet dangling from the rock, breaking up the hickory switch in his hand, the angels are looking on to see what he will decide ; or, if not angels, we know the great God is watching him. His omniscient eye sees all the consequences of each act, and He is never an indifferent spectator of such a conflict in a human heart.

Leonard had left home later than usual,

and the shadows had gathered over the grim hills; the last note of the wood-bird was quivering through the silence, and the lowing of the cows at the bars told him it was time for them to be released. Still the boy sat lost in thought, pushing his toes in and out of a crevice in the rock at his feet. But all at once he jumped down quickly, gave one look at the darkening sky, and rushed towards the bars, letting them down hastily.

"No, I won't do it! I'll be honest *through and through*, as grandfather says."

But, for all that, as he walked homeward, stroking the sides of his favourite heifer, a gush of hot tears poured down his cheeks. It was not easy to give up his cherished pleasure, and its promised delights rose up before him all the brighter now that they were beyond his reach. Beneath the sobs and the regret lay the consciousness of having done right, which helped him to bear the disappointment; but, in spite of that, it was a grievous disappointment, and he was making a great sacrifice for what he believed to be true and right.

Bear it bravely, my boy! You have taken a great step towards making yourself, for all coming time, an honest man, yea, more, an *honourable* man, whose soul shall scorn all deceptions and concealments, and cling to the truth,—the pure, unvarnished, holy truth, which God loves, and in which all holy beings in the universe delight.

When Leonard reached the gate, his father was standing by it. "Did you know the mill was running again, father?" he asked.

"Yes, I heard so," was the laconic answer.

"It would have done no good if I had tried to conceal it," was Leonard's first thought; and he was very glad he had not tried.

"Shall you want me to go to mill tomorrow afternoon?" was his next question.

"Yes."

That one short monosyllable settled Leonard's fate so far as the fishing-party was concerned. Had the father the slightest idea that his son's soul had been stirred to its very depths by a conflict between good and evil? Probably not; for George W. Roberts was one of those men who, upright and exemplary in all the business of life, seem to utterly forget that they were ever boys, and who never show the slightest sympathy with the trials or joys of their children. Leonard never spoke of it to any one: probably he never was aware himself that he had fought a battle and come off conqueror; yet it was written down in God's book of remembrance in imperishable lines,—

—"the conflict, and the victory too."

John was not at school Saturday forenoon: he stayed at home to welcome his friends, and was so much engrossed by them, that when Leonard stopped on his way home to tell him he could not go, he showed little surprise or grief. So no one but himself felt the disappointment; but he felt it keenly; and, as he walked homeward, it was all he could do to keep back the hot tears. And when he saw the whole party, soon after, driving by with their fishing-rods and baskets, looking so merry and gay, he gazed sorrowfully after them till they were quite out of sight, saying, bitterly, "I wish I could ever go, as other boys do, and have a good time!"

About two o'clock that afternoon, Leonard might be seen driving along that self-same road with his load of grain, on his way to the mill.

"How I pity him!" said Mabel, as he drove out of the yard. "I did so want he should go a-fishing."

"Yes, I wish he could have gone," said his mother, with a sigh.

Shall *we* pity him, gentle reader? We are greatly inclined to; but perhaps if we could read his future, and see how this and similar hardships made a man of him, —a self-relying, truthful, courageous man, who was never afraid to do right, never afraid of a little hardship, never afraid of standing up fearlessly for what he believed the truth,—we should rather congratulate him. The rough wind that shakes the little sapling pitilessly only roots it firmer in the soil, and gives it strength to shoot up into those fair and symmetrical proportions which the tenant of the sunny and sheltered enclosure can never reach. Let us not fear, then, to trust our young friend to the stern discipline of his life among the hills. Perhaps our pity might better be reserved for those whose wishes are all gratified, and who are not learning to control themselves or to bear disappointments bravely. To them the future may very likely bring the severest burdens.

Leonard had a cool, breezy ride to the mill, and a pleasant chat with the good-natured miller. When he returned at night, his mother and sisters had set the table in the yard, and, as a little treat, had baked him a strawberry short-cake, his favourite delicacy. And Mabel and Lucy had put on their pink-calico dresses in honor of the *picnic,* as they called it, and had trimmed the table with flowers from their garden, arranging every thing as prettily as they knew how. Little Sydney was enchanted at finding his plate encircled with a tiny wreath of myrtle-leaves and rose-buds, and it was all a very delightful surprise to Leonard. The little repast went off very merrily; and loud shouts of laughter might have been heard by any passer-by, showing how cheaply and easily young hearts may be made happy.

As Leonard was going to his little attic chamber that night, his mother laid her hand tenderly on his head. "You are a good boy, Leonard," she said, "and a great help and comfort to me;" and he saw a tear was in her eye.

Mrs. Roberts never lavished praises on

her children; and that one short commendation sent Leonard to his bed with a glowing cheek and grateful heart. Yes, with his mother's blessing resting on him, and w th the approbation of his own conscience, he was a happy boy that night,— even though he had been sadly disappointed, and had been to no pleasure-party, like other boys.

We think, too, that Leonard had now taken another step towards becoming a true patriot. We may be confident that the boy who could be thus true to his parents, and true to his conscience, will never be disloyal to his country in after-years. Loyal to parents, loyal to country, loyal to God,—this is the threefold loyalty which must constitute a Christian patriot; and such seeds sown in youth will surely spring up and in time bear glorious fruit.

## CHAPTER VIII.

#### SUNDAY IN THE RED HOUSE.

THE next day was one of those bright, beautiful Sundays in which earth, air and sky seem to unite in bringing a Sabbath stillness and purity into human souls. Sunday was kept in the good old-fashioned way at the red house; and so perfect was the stillness on this summer morning that the ticking of the clock in the kitchen and the occasional cackle of a hen in the yard sounded strangely loud and shrill. Every corner of the cottage had been put in exact order. The parents were sitting quietly, each by a window, reading the Bible, or some religious book; while the daughters studied their Sunday-school lessons. The mother had just heard Leonard and Sydney repeat their lessons, for even the latter belonged to a class, and regularly committed a few verses from the Testament to repeat to his teacher. Grandfather sat in a large arm-chair by the open door, and the two boys had seated themselves on the door-steps close by.

"Now show me the ark, grandfather," said Sydney, whose Sunday privilege it was to look at the pictures in the great Bible. The rude wood-cut, intended to represent the flood, had a long boat with a roof over it, at the door of which stood a man with his hand stretched out to take in a dove that was flying in the distance.

"Noah was such a good man, God didn't let him be drowned," said Sydney. "Was the dove a good dove too, grandfather?"

"Doves can't be good," exclaimed Leonard: "they haven't got any souls!"

"But doves *are* good," said Sydney: "ain't they, grandfather?"

"Not good in the same sense that boys and girls are, for they don't know right from wrong; but they are gentle and sweet-tempered, because God made them so."

"Is that such a ship as you used to sail in?" said Sydney.

"No, indeed: that was a great tall ship, with spars and masts,—a full-rigged whaler," answered his grandfather.

"Did you ever see a whale swallow a man up alive, grandfather?" was the child's next inquiry; for he was a persistent questioner.

"No: we hadn't any Jonahs aboard, I reckon," said the old gentleman, laughing.

"Now show me Moses in the bulrushes." After gazing some time, he said, "He was a pretty baby: wa'n't he, grandfather?"

"Yes, and he grew up a first-rate man," said Leonard.

"So he did,—just such a man as God loved and blessed; and so he made him a great captain over the army of the Israelites to lead them out of the land of bondage."

"Did they fight, grandfather?"

"Oh, yes, indeed, a great many battles; and God gave them the victory, because they were his own chosen people. Sometimes they were few in number, and their enemies numerous and powerful; but God was their leader, and he can subdue all the hosts of the wicked when he pleases: so he brought them to the promised land."

"Now show me Daniel and the lions." This was Sydney's favourite picture. The crouching attitude of the beasts just ready for a spring, their shaggy heads, with their wide-open mouths and white teeth, were very impressive; and over and over grandfather had been asked to tell him the story.

"Didn't he feel afraid when he heard the lions roar?"

"I guess not, because he was so sure God would take care of him. He had seen how his three friends came safe out of the fiery furnace, and I dare say he felt safe too; 'cause he knew he was a doin' right. A man may allers feel safe when he's a doin' his duty."

"Daniel was pretty bold," said Leonard, "or he wouldn't have dared to kneel down three times a day with all his windows open, after the king had said he would put any man into the lion's den who prayed to God."

"Yes," said their grandfather, "Daniel never was afraid to do his duty. When he was first brought before the king (and then he must have been quite young), the Bible says, 'he would not defile himself with the portion of the king's meat, nor with the wine which he drank.' He didn't begin life with doin' wrong for fear he should be laughed at; and, as I've said afore, *begin right when you're boys, if you want to come out right when you're men.* Habits are amazin' powerful things; and afore you know it, they're coiled up all round you so tight and fast you can't get away from 'em."

"*I* mean to begin right," said Leonard,

complacently. "I am going to always tell the truth, and to stand up for what is right. Some boys think it's foolish to be so particular; but Miss Brace says everybody should be honest, even in their looks."

"That's good doctrine," said the old gentleman. "I guess Miss Brace is the right kind of a schoolma'am. But you won't allers find it's so easy to do exactly right as you think, Leonard: you'll come to some tough places where you'll be hard pushed, and where the way will be all hedged up before you."

"But nobody can make me do wrong, if I don't choose to."

"That is true; but that's just where the trouble is. Human natur' is a curi's thing, —a dreadful unsartin thing. A man makes up his mind exactly what he'll do, and then, when he's the surest he's goin' to do it, like as not he goes and does exactly what he didn't mean to. Now, he ain't forced to do it agin his will, but his will itself shifts about: he chooses to do right one minute, and the next minute some temptation comes, and he chooses to do wrong."

"Yes," he added, musingly, "it ain't easy to allers do what we ought to, and none of us get through this world without findin' out we are poor weak critturs and need a deal of help. What was it made Daniel so full of courage? Because he prayed to God to help him; and God did help him. 'Tain't likely, boys, you'll ever have to go into a den of lions; but if you live you'll come to places where you'll have to either commit a sin or face something about as terrible as a roarin' lion. Nobody travels to heaven through such a world as this without havin' to fight his way. I shall be dead and gone then; but remember your old grandfather told you never to be afraid of any thing but doin' wrong. Allers keep up a good heart if you are doin' right; and when you come to a tight place, ask God to carry you through it, and go forward and do your duty like a man. God will be just as near to you as he was to Daniel, and just as ready to help you, if you only call on him. You can't keep yourself in the right path a single day, but he can allers keep you, in this world and in the world to come. I'm an old man now, but I put myself into the Lord's keepin' when I was a boy, and he's never failed me, and he never will. I shall go out of this world pretty soon, but I can't go where he won't be there to take care of me. He's kept me safe for over seventy years, in storm and calm, in battle and shipwreck, on the sea and on the land, and I ain't none afraid to trust him a little longer. Yes," he said, raising his eyes reverently to the serene heavens, "'I know whom I have believed, and am persuaded that He is able to keep that which I have committed to him against that day.'"

At nine o'clock the old church-bell rang out sweet and clear over all the hills, inviting old and young to the house of prayer. Then each member of the family went to his room to put on the clean Sunday suit which the careful mother had in readiness: the horse was harnessed to the two-seated wagon, the slight lunch, of crackers and doughnuts, was rolled up and by ten o'clock all were ready to leave the house. The doors and windows were carefully closed,— for fear of showers, not of thieves; for the cottages stood all over those lonely hills, gleaming out here and there in the soft sunshine of that summer morning, and each was left unlocked without a thought of danger, though all were tenantless save where some aged person too infirm or some child too young to go to church remained behind.

Grandfather drove, and the mother, daughters and little Sydney rode, while the father and Leonard walked on ahead. They, and indeed most of the congregation, who came from still greater distances, stayed through the short intermission at noon, the younger and middle-aged persons going into the Sunday-school, while the elderly ones sat in the porch or on the steps, or wandered out into the graveyard close by, talking in subdued tones to one another. At one, the afternoon bell summoned them to their pews again, and by half-past two they were all on their way home. It was a pretty sight to see the long rows of wagons winding up the steep hills which rose in each direction from the little green on which the church stood, and watch them separating at the different turnings of the road, each to seek a quiet dwelling among the hills. All the air was hushed, and full of such sweet repose as only can be found on a bright Sabbath afternoon, when God seems to draw visibly nearer to the world he has created than on other days, and bathe it in light and joy.

Mrs. Roberts, as was the custom then and is now in such scattered towns, had her principal meal about four o'clock on Sunday afternoon. Something a little nicer than usual was then prepared, though always something which had been mostly cooked the day before, and so required little labour on the Sabbath, save the boiling of the tea-kettle for the cup of strong tea then so popular in New England farm-houses. The long fast insured a keen appetite, and they all (especially the children) greatly enjoyed this Sunday dinner, or supper, as they called it. Some might be inclined to frown on this indulgence as unsuited to the day. Not so Mary Roberts. She wanted Sunday to be a cheerful and pleasant day to her family, and thought there was no harm in the temperate enjoyment of a nice, simple meal. Was it not God's gift, and, though a lesser blessing than the spiritual food bestowed on that day, still a blessing, to be gratefully received and enjoyed with glad hearts?

After this meal there came a long interval before dark. Mrs. Roberts knew this interval was in too many households one of tedious yawning, or anxious watching for the disappearance of the sun; and she had tried to make it to her children one of the happiest of the week. It was almost the only time in her busy life when she could gather her children around her, and her face was never so bright, so beaming with tenderness and love, as when she sat down with them all about her for a Sunday-afternoon talk. Her face never looked gloomy when she spoke of Jesus and heaven, but lighted up into a sweet radiance at the thought of that Friend and that home so precious to her soul. Bible-stories in her language became sweet and attractive to her children, and that quiet, beautiful Sabbath twilight was the sweetest hour of the week to even the youngest of them. The "best room," seldom used during the week, was always opened then, and the family assembled in it. It was a very nice-looking, pleasant apartment, with its fringed white curtains, and woodbine creepers shading the windows, and not in the least stiff and gloomy, as "best rooms" sometimes are. The children's books and pictures were all kept there, and on Sundays there were always vases of flowers on the table and mantel-shelf in summer, and of the beautiful evergreen laurel in winter, giving the room a cheery look. To be sure, there was only a home-made carpet on the floor, and plain chairs and table, and a calico-covered lounge, also of home manufacture; but each article was as pleasing to the eyes of those simply-trained children as if made of rosewood and damask. The most noticeable thing in this little room was a cabinet of shells and other foreign curiosities. It had been brought on his return-voyage from the Pacific islands years ago by Captain Roberts to his wife and children. There were shells of all sizes, forms and colours in it, with ostrich-eggs, feathers of brilliant hues, curious girdles of cocoa-nut-leaves, and little sandal-wood boxes and screens, with some hideous little idols of stone and wood. The tropical odour of the sandal-wood could be perceived the moment you entered the room, and it would doubtless through life be associated with Sunday afternoons in the minds of the children, however widely they might wander from the old red house.

These curiosities were an unfailing source of entertainment to the children, and many a sweet lesson of God's love and care had they helped the mother to impress on their tender minds. There was a vein of poetry slumbering in Mary Roberts's soul; and when the children held those beautifully spotted sea-shells to their ear, listening to that mysterious swell of the ocean-waves which seemed to be still lingering within them, or looked at the plumage of some rare tropical bird, she told them many a sweet, thrilling story of the sea, and the lonely islands that lie upon it; and, quickened by the magic power of her voice and eye, these stories became links to bind their souls in a closer union to nature and nature's God; for she had the rare art to make each story teach some lesson of faith in God or love to man. Grandfather too, had stories to tell them,—sometimes from the Bible and sometimes from his own experience. And when the daughters grew older, they each, like their mother, had a sweet voice for singing; and this was an added Sunday pleasure, in which even their father joined with his full bass notes. No, Sunday was never a dull day in Mr. Roberts's house, nor was it ever a day like other days; but it was set apart and consecrated by far holier thoughts and purer pleasures than marked the other six.

## CHAPTER IX.

### SUNDAY EVENING.

THE sun had set in cloudless splendour, and a bright new moon now showed her silver crescent in the west; but the air was so soft and balmy that the grandfather, the mother and Leonard still lingered at the open door. Sydney had been put to bed. Mr. Roberts had himself gone for the cows that night, and milked them; and Mabel and Lucy were attending to straining the milk, and other necessary duties, in the kitchen; while the three sat quietly at the door, watching the stars as they

> "Came twinkling one by one
> Upon the shady sky."

To one accustomed to the life of a large town or city, the "silence that was on the lonely hills" at this hour would have been oppressive; but it was not so to those quiet watchers. To their eyes, every feature in the landscape was familiar; each outline of the dusky hills, each tree that stood up against the sky in the distance like some shadowy giant, each rounded hillock, and even each bush and rock and tuft of wild flowers, was something pleasant to their eyes, and wore a friendly look. They were familiar, too, with that wide sweep of the heavens above, and knew where to look for each different group of stars, though ignorant of the names science has given to them. To the old sailor especially, who had for years watched them from the deck of his vessel as it ploughed through the foaming billows, they were full of interest; for they had been his guides and companions in many a midnight hour when he kept watch on deck amid the solitude of the vast ocean; and he gazed at them now with an emotion which no mere landsman could well understand.

"There is something about the stars

which allers makes a body serious," he said, breaking a long silence. "When I fust went to sea, I was as thoughtless a chap as ever lived. But when it came my turn to take the watch, and I used to lay on deck, seein' nothing round me but the dark water below, and the great sky above, full of shinin' stars, curi's ideas used to come into my head. I wondered if God's eye wa'n't up there among the stars, lookin' straight down into my soul; and all the things my mother had told me about God, and heaven, and hell, would rise up before me and make me tremble. When I lay there in the clear, still nights, alone out on the great ocean, I felt as if God was somehow nearer to me than on the land; but I was afraid of him, and didn't like to think about him. The second time I sailed, there was a young lad aboard,—a kind of weakly boy he was,—who'd been sent on the voyage for his health. We was on a fishin'-smack then, bound for the Great Banks, to get cod. This lad—mabbe he was sixteen or seventeen years of age—used sometimes to sit in one corner by himself and read his Bible. He was most allers brisk and lively and full of fun, for all he looked so sickly; but once in a while he seemed sad and homesick. One day he told me how he had a mother who was a widow, and how he was her only child. 'And I'm afraid,' says he, 'that if any thing was to happen to me it would almost break her heart.'

"I didn't wonder; for he had such a takin' way with him, that all on board loved him and would do any thing in the world to please him. He liked to talk to us boys, and took a deal of interest in seein' how we fixed our lines and bait to fish with. It was all kind o' new to him; and he'd ask the drollest questions you ever heerd, for he was dreadful ignorant about all such things. Sometimes Gilbert (Gilbert Watson was his name) would come and sit on deck with me when it was so hot at night he couldn't sleep below;

and then he too would look at the stars, and tell me what he'd read in books about 'em, and how some of 'em was great worlds, a great deal bigger than our world, and what names they was all called by; for he had a store of book-larnin', though he was so amazin' ignorant of some things; and then he would talk to me as good and pious as any minister.

"'What a mighty being God must be,' he said, one night, 'to make all these great worlds, and keep 'em all a movin' exactly right! I wonder if anybody is livin' in them, and, if there is, what kind of folks they are.' 'Tom,' said he, looking up at me with his great bright eyes, 'Tom, perhaps we shall go and live in one of the stars when we die: don't you think we shall?' Now, I was a great, rough, lubberly boy, strong and hearty, and I didn't like to think about dyin', any way: so I said, 'I don't know nothin' about sich things. What *I* think about is how I'm goin' to get along in this world, and where

I shall go, and what I shall see. I mean to live to be a captain,' says I, 'and sail all over the world, before I die.' I can see now just how he looked when I said that, as well as if he stood right by me this very minute. He was sittin' on a coil of rope that lay on deck, and he smiled a little,—a sort of sad smile it was,—and says he,—

"'I hope you will, Tom; but I don't expect to live to be a man.'

"'Pshaw! nonsense!' says I: 'don't go to bein' vapoury and notional. We shall see you runnin' up to the mast-head like a cat, yet.' He'd been put under the cap'n's care, and if he got strong he was to learn how to handle the ropes like the other boys. But he shook his head. 'No, Tom,' says he, quietly, 'I don't think I shall ever see home again.' It made me all of a tremble to hear him say that; but I tried to laugh, and told him he shouldn't be thinkin' of such a thing. He didn't much heed what I said, but went on in his quiet way:—'I wouldn't care so much if it wasn't for my mother: I don't feel afraid to die.' I tried to make an answer, but I couldn't; for there was something a stickin' in my throat. 'No, I'm not afraid to die, Tom,' says he, 'because I know God can take care of me in another world just as well as he can in this; and I want you should trust God too, Tom. You don't swear, like the other boys; and I want you should love God with all your heart, and serve him.'

"'I don't know much about God,' said I,—I was 'most a-cryin';—'I allers feel afraid to think much about him.'

"'He *is* a great and powerful God,' said he; 'and if he hadn't sent Jesus Christ into the world to save us, and so show how much he loves us, we might all be afraid to think about him; but Jesus was all love and kindness; and he is the very image of God; and it is through him we are to come to God and learn what God s. He died to save us, and he will save us if we seek him and believe in him. If you will only believe in Christ and become his disciple, then you need not feel afraid to live, nor afraid to die either. Haven't you got a Bible, Tom?' he asked.

"'No,' I said; 'mother gave me one, but I've lost it.'

"He thought a minute, and then said, 'If any thing happens to me, Tom, I want you to have my Bible, and to read in it every day.' I couldn't help crying when he said this.

"'Oh, don't cry,' said he, smiling: "may-be nothing will happen; perhaps I shall grow up to be a stout and healthy man yet; but you must read the Bible all the same, Tom, for we need that to tell us how to live, as well as how to die.'

"Pretty soon he got sleepy, and went down; but the next day he brought me a little Testament he took from the purser's office.

"Soon after this, he began to gain. He'd more colour in his face, and didn't cough so hard; and when we got to the Banks he used to help us fish, and began to look real tough and hearty; and I says to myself, 'Gilbert will be as well as anybody yet.' So it went on for some weeks; but when we turned towards home, he seemed to droop a little. One night, when we was a'most home, and were all on the look-out for land ahead, somebody come in the middle of the night and called me to go down to the cap'n's room; and there I found Gilbert lyin', just as white as a sheet, and lookin' as if he was quite dead. He had been took all of a sudden raisin' blood, and the cap'n had carried him down to his own room, thinkin' he'd be more comfortable there. He opened his eyes and smiled a little when he saw me standin' by him, but he couldn't speak, and pretty soon he shut 'em up again, and went to sleep. He never opened 'em after that, but just lay there still and quiet as a baby, breathin' softly, till four o'clock the next afternoon, when his breath stopped, and he was gone."

The old man paused, and wiped a tear from his eye.

"Yes, he was gone! There wa'n't a man among us, even the roughest, swearin'est sailor we had aboard, but shed a tear when they went to look at him, he looked so beautiful and smilin', lyin' there as'eep."

"Did they bury him in the ocean?" asked Mrs. Roberts, softly.

"No: we got sight o' land that very mornin', and the cap'n said he would try to keep him, so his mother could have one more look at him. They put all his things up nicely, and in his Bible they found a little slip of paper, on which was wrote, '*To be given to Tom, who I know will read it for my sake.*' The cap'n brought it to me himself, and I cried jist like a baby: I couldn't help it! I've got that Bible now," said the old man, wiping his eyes, " and that bit of paper is still a-lyin' in it. I never failed to read in't after that, if it wa'n't but a single verse. Sometimes the fellows used to laugh at me; but I didn't mind 'em, for I could see Gilbert's pale face right before me, and hear him sayin', '*You'll read it for my sake.*' I thank God I parsevered; for out of that Bible I larnt the way of salvation, and I hope God has given me strength to walk in it ever since. I have wanted it to live by, as Gilbert said; and now I can say, as he did sixty years ago, sittin' there on that bunch of rope away out on the Atlantic Ocean, 'I am not afraid to die; for God can keep me in another world just as well as he can in this.'

"But," continued the old man, "I never see the stars shinin' out so bright and clear, without thinkin' on him. Mabbe he is livin' up among 'em, as he said. Sometimes I used to think he was, and that he could look down and see me when I kept watch on deck such still, clear nights as this. But we don't know where the sperit goes: we only know God makes it one of the happy, rejoicin' sperits round his throne."

"Did you ever hear from his poor mother?" said Mrs. Roberts.

"Why,—it was very strange, but when we got to land and inquired about her, we found she died about a month before he did, and of consumption too. He told me once she was always weakly. The cap'n went on himself with the body, and he see him buried in the little graveyard, right beside his mother. He said he couldn't help rejoicin' that she wasn't there to hear about his death; for she was such a good Christian woman, nobody doubted she had gone to a better world to meet her boy."

"A world where 'God shall wipe away all tears from their eyes, and there shall be no more death, neither sorrow nor crying,'" said Mrs. Roberts, softly.

Leonard had not spoken, but he had listened attentively to the little narrative; and now he went silently into the house, and to his room. Perhaps he too, when he looked at the bright stars, would think of the young lad who had watched them so long ago and then passed away to be with God. He asked his grandfather, a few Sundays afterwards, to show him the Bible that had been given to him; and he looked very thoughtfully at it, and at the slip of paper, now yellow and worn with age. "You may have it for your own, Leonard," said his grandfather; "and may the God who blessed that dear youth —the God of your fathers—be your God." He turned to the sixth chapter of Numbers, and with a trembling hand drew a line beneath the words which God commanded Moses to give to Aaron and his sons as words of blessing for the children of Israel:—

"*The Lord bless thee, and keep thee, the Lord make his face shine upon thee, and be gracious unto thee; the Lord lift up his countenance upon thee, and give thee peace."*

"This is what I wish for you, my boy," he said. "Don't lose this book; and, when you look at it in comin' years, 'twill put you in mind of me, and of him who owned it first,—the dear young lad who died at sea."

## CHAPTER X.

### THE TOWN-MEETING.

THE leaves which shaded Mr. Roberts's house through the summer-heats brightened into autumnal tints, and then were swept away by the fierce north winds, till the bare trees stood shivering in the November frosts. The harvests had all been gathered in, and a time of comparative leisure was drawing nigh. The first Tuesday of November was town-meeting day in Woodlee,—indeed, in all the United States; for it was the year for choosing Presidential electors. There had been an unusually exciting campaign throughout the land, and voters were expected to assemble in full force in every city, town and village.

"It's such a windy day, I'm afraid you

will take cold," said Mrs. Roberts, when she saw grandfather preparing himself to go.

"Pshaw! I ain't so far gone yet that I can't stand a land-gale," answered the old gentleman, somewhat impatiently, for he had an old man's aversion to being considered feeble. "I've voted for President nine times, and I must try the tenth. It's worth something to have tried ten times to give the country a good President," he added, smiling.

"Who did you vote for first?" asked Lucy.

"*Who?* Why, for George Washington, the Lord be praised! I wish we had a man among us now I could feel as sure of as I did of him!"

"Everybody liked him, I suppose," said Mabel.

"No, not everybody. Some folks at that time were afraid of him, and afraid of every thing, and found fault with every thing, just as some do now. You see,

## A GREAT CHANGE. 141

we'd only just got started then; and they couldn't tell exactly how the Constitution was goin' to work, till it was tried. Some thought it gave the people too much liberty, and some thought it didn't give 'em enough; and the fearful ones said we should drift into a monarchy, as sure as could be. We was a small nation then, —small and weak too; but God presarved us among all the tumults and commotions of that day, and now we've got to be a great and prosperous people. Our rulers need a deal of wisdom, and of the fear of God, to fit 'em to rule such a nation as we are now."

John Hall had stopped for Leonard; for of course all the boys would congregate in the centre of the town to get their share of excitement on election-day; and both were in high spirits.

"You boys think it's great fun to go to town-meetin' now," said the grandfather; "but one of these days you'll have to make a more earnest business of it. Like enough you'll vote a dozen times for President. Now, I charge you to see to it that you allers vote for a man who's honest and true to his country, who fears God and keeps his commandments. It's a great thing to choose your own rulers; but, if you choose bad ones, it's a curse, instead of a blessin', to be allowed to vote."

Both boys assured him they should always vote for the very best man there was in the whole United States. Little did they dream of the difficulties which might lie in the way, making it far from easy to know who is the best man even among rival candidates, or to vote for him when known.

They rode to the village together,—the old man, his son, and the boys. The meeting was held in the church, as was then common in most small towns. It was curious to watch those independent voters as they drove up by wagon-loads from all parts of the scattered township, every man coming who could possibly hobble from the wagon to the door, and some who needed help to do even that. All were excited and talkative; and they drew off in little groups as their political affinities united them. Each man's mind was fully made up as to which of the candidates to vote for; for, however the uneducated foreigners who come to the polls in our large cities may be influenced by motives brought to bear upon them on election-day, there was not one in that rural town but had heard the merits of the rival candidates discussed in neighbourhood gatherings, in village caucuses, as well as in the newspapers, till he had ideas of his own in reference to the policy which would be adopted by each of them, and had formed in his own mind a settled preference for one or the other of them.

To a thoughtful observer, few sights are more deeply interesting than that of a body of voters assembled in town-meeting. As they stand there, some of them coarsely—most of them plainly—dressed, with faces bronzed by exposure and hands hardened by toil, he cannot but remember that by these and such as these the destinies of one of the most powerful governments in the world are to be decided, and that according as they are true or false to the great interests of freedom will this great nation preserve or lose its liberties. How ardently a true lover of his country longs to inspire each of these voters with a love of justice, a devotion to freedom, and a proper sense of his responsibility! Then, and then only, could he feel that our country would be safe! Oh, if ever a man should cleanse his soul from all that is false, mean and degrading, if ever he should have clean hands and a pure heart, ever lift on high a petition for Divine guidance, it is when he goes to the ballot-box; for the act of voting must involve either good or evil to his whole country, now and in the future. It is a proud thing to be able to vote for the Chief Magistrate of these United States, and a man has a right to hold his head higher and to tread firmer on this than on other days; but it is also a very solemn thing; for each individual vote affects the grand result. Think, then, of your responsibilities, ponder them seriously, ye whose prerogative it is to vote; and in future may God help you to vote wisely, uprightly and in his most holy fear!

Only purify *your* hearts, ye who go to the ballot-box, and make *your* hands clean, and you will soon have no occasion to complain of corruption among your rulers; for your rulers, your legislators, and all your office-holders, from the highest to the lowest, are of just the stamp you ordain; and if they are faithless to their trust, you are responsible for their short-comings!

The clergyman of Woodlee opened the meeting with prayer, and then the voting went on quietly, the polls being kept open till sundown, as by law provided. Outside, the boys were somewhat noisy, having engaged in boisterous sports in the interval of waiting; but the older population were orderly and quiet. Few went to their homes till the votes were counted; and if there followed some undue exhilaration among the prevailing party, some uproarious cheers and rough joking, to the honour of Woodlee be it spoken, there was little of intemperance or profaneness on this day of unbounded license. By dark all had dispersed to their homes, save a dozen or two still left standing on the village-green, and a dozen or two more in the bar-room of the little inn.

Mrs. Roberts had a hot supper ready for the voters on their return; for she knew some neighbour (as they called those living two or three miles farther from the Centre) would be sure to drop in to eat with them and to talk over the events of the day. And so it proved. Deacon Price and neighbour Warren, the latter as old as Captain Roberts, and, like him, an emigrant from Eastern Massachusetts in his younger days, stopped to partake of some of Mrs. Roberts's stewed chicken and hot biscuits, and to drink three or four of the cups which "cheer but not inebriate." They grew lively and jolly under the combined influence of good fare and good company, and told their merriest anecdotes and longest stories as they sat around the blazing fire, while the November wind whistled unheeded outside the little cottage-windows.

Mrs. Roberts and her daughters, each of whom read the papers with eagerness and had her own opinions on political questions, listened intently to their conversation; and even Sydney was allowed to sit up later than usual, to enjoy the merriment. But when eight o'clock came, the two guests departed: the family circle drew closer around the fire, and by degrees their conversation took a graver character.

"I've cast my last vote for President," said the grandfather, after he had been silently looking into a bed of coals for some minutes. "Four years hence, younger folks will have to do the votin'."

"Oh, perhaps not," said his daughter.

"You are very active yet, and younger now than most men at sixty."

"The Lord has blessed me with good health all my life, 'tis true; but I'm breakin' up, Mary. I feel it sensibly, of late. I don't mean to be anxious about the future. The Lord's time is the best time, and in his time I shall go, and not before. But I can't help thinkin' a good deal about the country, George. I can't help feelin' as though there was risin' up among us a bad set of notions. Folks are gettin' too greedy for office, too fond of change, and they put men into office that ain't fit for it; and there ain't the reverence felt for those in authority that there used to be and ought to be."

"The last follows from the first, father," answered George. "How *can* we respect such men as hold office now?'

"But they are such men as we put in ourselves," said his father.

"I know that," said George, sharply, "and that's the worst of it. But who believes the men we send to our Legislature now are fit to make laws for us?"

"And if we send men to make laws that we don't respect, pretty soon there'll be no respect for the laws they make," said the father, "and when the laws ain't respected, a country like our's is ruined; for we've nothin' else to govern us. No, nothin' but the laws! You young folks, then, must see to this. You must see that good men are put in office,—not only smart men, but upright, honest men, with consciences that can't be warped or twisted. Why, an unprincipled man in office is jist as bad as a rotten plank in a ship at sea: it may be tucked out of sight and covered up by others atop of it, but there's a weak spot there, and whenever there comes a strain on the vessel it will be sure to show itself; and if you get many good-for-nothing timbers into her, she'll jist as sartainly go to pieces as there comes a gale. You can't save a vessel that's made up of rotten timbers,—no, nor a nation that's ruled by wicked men! Every town-officer you choose, if he's a scamp, weakens the ship of state a little; and so on up to the highest in the land. So, I say, don't let us have any rotten timber *anywhere!* I'm a'most done with these things myself; but do you, George, try all you can to keep such men out; not only vote agin 'em, but use all your influence to make others vote agin 'em too, and to keep every man who's corrupt from havin' any thing to do either in makin' the laws for us or in administerin' 'em after they are made. That's your fust duty as a good citizen and a Christian man; and every voter who don't do this commits a sin in the sight of God, and will have to answer for it in the judgment-day."

This idea seemed to dwell on his mind; for he returned to it again.

"Some folks think," said he, "that if a man's only of their party, that's enough; but I tell you it ain't enough. There must be integrity in the man, or you can't depend on him; and that must be a poor party, truly, that can't find among it men enough for candidates who are both able and honest In our country there's fewer checks on the people who hold office, and on the people who put 'em in, than in any other; and because we've got so much more libbaty and freedom, we must have just so much more vartue and integrity; for it's integrity—it's *integrity*, I tell you —that's to presarve us. If we lose that, we are a ruined people!"

"Do you think there is as much integrity among the people now as there was formerly?" asked Mrs. Roberts.

"Well, it's a pretty hard thing to tell. It does seem to me there ain't; but then old folks allers think old times and old ways was best. It's nateral to 'em. In old times there might be more drinkin' and swearin' than there is now, but there wa'n't nigh so much cheatin' and lyin'. When Jefferson come in President, a great many good folks thought the Evil One himself had got the upper hand, and that the country would sartainly go right to ruin; but it didn't. There was a sight o' wickedness in the country then, and there's a sight now, and it's hard to say which is the worst. But I've allers thought the Lord raised up this country to do a great work in the world; and, if he did, she'll do it. No nation, nor all the nations of the world, can't stop it. Yes, I love my country—this blessed Union, and the blessed old flag—better than any thing on airth; but I don't feel afraid to trust 'em all in the Lord's hands. May he make the dear old stars and stripes a praise and a glory to all comin' generations, and grant that neither my children, nor children's children, may ever live to see 'em disgraced or trampled on!"

At prayers, that night, the heart of the old man was kindled into unwonted fervour, and the petitions he poured out for the country and those who should rule over it were prompted by emotions which seemed vainly struggling for expression. It was a prayer never forgotten by those who heard it; and long years afterwards it rose up vividly in their remembrance, kindling a new glow of patriotic feeling and devotion to the country their fathers had loved so well and prayed for so earnestly.

## CHAPTER XI.

### SLEEP.

It was ten o'clock when the family retired that night,—a late hour for the inmates of the Roberts's family. Out of the sitting-room two doors opened into two sleeping-rooms, and these were occupied one by the father and mother and the other by the grandfather. The door between these rooms was always left open, so that assistance could be promptly rendered if any should be needed.

But there was no call that night. No groan nor sigh was heard, as hour after hour of the long autumn night passed away. The mother was awake more than once, but all was silent, save the moaning of the wind. Yet in those still night-watches the Angel of Death entered that humble abode, and bore away the spirit of him who had so long dwelt within it, —bore it away, tenderly, noiselessly, to the bosom of its God; and he whose last act had been one of faithful service to his country, whose last words had been words of intercession before God's throne in its behalf, had passed beyond the boundaries of space and time, to inhabit "a better country, even an heavenly."

It did not seem possible he could be gone; and yet it was true. The dear grandfather, whom they all loved so tenderly, was found lying in his bed, his face as calm and tranquil as a child's, but life had forever fled! How or when the spirit had departed, could never be known. That there had been no suffering was evident from the position of the body and the composure of every feature; but *where* it had gone, no one for an instant doubted. As the dawn lighted up the eastern sky, they knew that a glorious and immortal morning was breaking in upon his soul, and that henceforth he would rejoice in the uncreated, ineffable light of God's countenance for evermore.

It was a sore bereavement. Every member of the family, even to the youngest child, had loved "grandpa," and turned to him for sympathy and counsel; for, though old in years, his heart had still kept young and fresh. No one else could ever be to them what he was, and no other words ever have the same charm for them as his quaint, old-fashioned words of counsel and reproof.

It was on one of those mild, Indian-summer days which November sometimes brings, that the mourning household, followed by a long procession of neighbours and friends, went to the little graveyard near the church to lay down their dead. Not a cloud rested on the sky, not a breath of wind stirred the few brown withered leaves which still clung to the trees; but a calm, radiant glory rested on all the hills as they passed by. He was laid beside the wife of his youth, "in the sure and certain hope of resurrection to everlasting life," there to slumber till all that are in their graves shall "hear the voice of the Son of man, and shall come forth, they that have done good unto the resurrection of life, and they that have done evil unto the resurrection of damnation."

Leonard wept at the grave long and bitterly. He was the especial favourite of his grandfather, and he had loved him in return with all the warmth of his boyish nature. It was his first bereavement, and "he refused to be comforted." But that night, when all was over, and he stood looking up at the quiet stars which were out in all their glory, moving on in their serene march through the silent heavens, his soul was calmed. He felt a new sense of the soul's immortality: he believed his beloved friend was alive still, —alive and happy,—perhaps was still remembering him in the new life he was living in the heavens. To him, as to his grandfather so many long years before, it seemed as if the eye of the departed might be gazing at him from those far-off worlds; and his heart thrilled with a vague but sincere desire to become pure and holy like those dear lost ones.

A boy's grief, though violent, is seldom enduring; and Leonard, though he never lost a venerating memory of what his grandfather had been to him, was soon occupied again by the cares and pleasures of his daily life.

But from that night he began to read daily in the little Bible which his grandfather had given him, and which was hallowed by so many touching associations. Often, too, as he grew older, some expression of his grandfather's would occur to him,—some quaint comparison, or some bit of advice, homely but sensible, which affected him as nothing else did. Especially did he cherish the old flag with an almost superstitious reverence, always unrolling it on each successive Fourth of

July; for he could never forget the look with which the aged patriot had said,—

"Mind, when grandfather's gone, you don't forget to set the old flag a-wavin' on the Fourth: 'pears to me it would do me good to see it even in another world."

## CHAPTER XII.

### TEN YEARS LATER.

Nowhere would the years be expected to slip away more quietly, leaving fewer traces of their flight, than in that humble dwelling at Woodlee; yet when we revisit it after ten years have fled, we shall find marked changes there. The outward aspect is much the same, save that the trees are taller and the fences older. If we enter the house at evening, we shall find the family assembled around the fire, the mother sitting in her old place, not greatly altered, though if we observe her closely we shall find there are deeper lines on her face and that her hair is becoming white and silvery. But Mary Roberts is now a widow; and for four years she has stood at the head of her household, with no strong arm to lean on but His who is the God of the widow and the fatherless.

The young man in the opposite corner must be our old friend Leonard; but how changed! We left him a boy, and now he is a man. He is not very tall, but his stout, muscular frame makes him look manly and older even than he is. He has the same dark-gray eyes, but the features are better harmonized, and he is now a sensible, good-looking young man of twenty,—by no means handsome, but with a decided, straightforward expression which makes one feel that he has opinions of his own, which he will not be likely to give up on any slight occasion. "A young man of character," you would be likely to say at first sight; and he looks, too, like one who has early felt responsibility and care. His face and hands show that he is a labouring man; but his whole bearing indicates intelligence and self-respect, as every labouring man's should; for who is more truly independent?

The sedate, composed-looking woman of twenty-six who sits by the table sewing, is the fair young Mabel of other days, grown mature and thoughtful; but the same bright smile lights up her face as she says,—

"I knew he would get the prize. The truth is, it costs Sydney nothing to excel in his studies. He learns so easily, study is only a delight to him."

"I hope he hasn't been sitting up late nights," said the careful mother. "Does he say any thing about his health?"

"No, nor about any thing else, only that he's got the prize, and that it made him half ashamed to take it, when he saw how disappointed Bascom was. Bascom, he says, had really studied harder than he, and better deserved to get it."

"That's just like Sydney," said Mabel, —"always thinking better of others than of himself."

"Yes, he's a modest little fellow as ever lived," said Leonard; "and he's a splendid scholar. He ought to keep right on with his studies. We must try to manage it, somehow."

"I know we can," said Mabel, eagerly; "at least to send him through this year."

"Don't be too sure of that," said the mother. "It would be pleasant to do it, but you mustn't be governed too much by feeling. If he is away in summer you'll be obliged to hire a man; and that takes off a great deal of the profits of the farm. Then Sydney's board-bill runs up pretty fast. I want him to stay there as much as you do, but I really doubt if it's best. There are a good many extra expenses on the farm this year, you know. The barn must be shingled, and a new front fence made; and we must not get into debt."

"No, indeed!" said Leonard, decidedly. The remembrance of the old debt which in his childhood had hung like a millstone on the family was a wholesome caution against becoming encumbered by another.

The question was whether Sydney, now

in his sixteenth year, should be kept at an academy in a neighbouring town where he had been studying through the winter. His fine scholarship and comparative inefficiency in all kinds of manual labour, had made it manifest that he was to get his living by brain-work of some kind. He had acquired all the branches taught in the district-schools of Woodlee rapidly and thoroughly, and a few more terms at the academy would fit him—for college? Yes; but, alas! that was not to be thought of. To fit him for teaching was all they dared look forward to. In that way he might support himself, and perhaps, as his own ardent, hopeful spirit whispered, carry himself in time through college and a profession.

George Roberts had lived to pay off the last instalment of the debt which had so long hung like an incubus upon him, and he was just beginning to take more hopeful and kindly views of life, when he was summoned away from it. During his last illness, he was able to give but few directions about his business affairs; and on Leonard, then only sixteen, had come the chief burden of supporting the family, so far as it was possible for such a boy to do it. It had been necessary to hire help, and the farm had not thrived as it did under his father's management; for, though George Roberts had been a melancholy, austere man, he was an excellent manager, and was universally respected for his uprightness and thorough integrity. Leonard was just beginning to appreciate the worth of his character and counsels when he was left fatherless. By the strictest economy the family had been kept together, and the farm saved for them free of debt; and, now that Leonard was older, their prospects had brightened somewhat. Lucy had married two years before, and gone West to live. They heard from her but seldom, and on the mother's heart there weighed a vague, unexpressed fear that she had not married satisfactorily, though she knew nothing positively unfavourable about her son-in-law's character or condition.

"It won't hurt Sydney to be out of school till winter," said the mother: "indeed, I think it will be better for him. He needs to have some hardships. He must be toughened a little before he will be able to make his own way in the world, as he's got to do."

"He don't help much on the farm," said Leonard, hesitatingly; "at least, we shall have to keep a man all the same."

"But he ought to help," said the mother, energetically. "Why, Leonard, he's as old now, into a month or two, as you were when your father died."

"Yes, but he's so different, mother. He's not strong, as I was, and——"

"And he doesn't like to work on a farm. I know that; but I think it's all wrong in him, and that he ought to do what he doesn't like to, as well as the rest of us."

"But I do like to work. I am just made up for a plodding farmer and nothing else.

Oh, mother," said Leonard, looking up earnestly into his mother's face, "you don't know how I've often had to struggle with a wicked, envious feeling in my heart towards Sydney. He's so gifted, so brilliant, and so sure to make his way in the world, and be looked up to and admired without working, while I shall always have to drudge and be nobody. Somehow, it didn't seem right or fair. But, mother," he added, cheerily, "don't look so troubled: it's all over now. Since last fall I've come to feel that we are all just in the right place, and can all be useful and happy wherever we are."

"*Since last fall!*" At that time a change had come over Leonard's purposes and the governing motive of his life. He had then professed himself a disciple of Jesus Christ; and for him to profess to be a disciple was to be one in reality, and to have his hopes, affections and acts brought into conformity to the will of his divine Master. It was, as the apostle expresses it, "to live in newness of life." His outward conduct was not so much changed as his inward purposes,—his ideas of life and duty. These had righted themselves, so to speak, and he saw them now from the true standpoint and in their just relations. Trained, as we have seen, to habits of thorough integrity towards man, he had now, by divine assistance, become honest also towards God, giving Him his due,—the affections of his heart and the service of his hands; honest also towards his own soul, not defrauding it of its birthright,— the elevation, the nobility, the true pleasures which rightfully belonged to it, and which it could never find but in a spiritual union to its Creator and Redeemer.

"Yes," continued Leonard, "I found all kinds of wrong, wicked feelings were coming up in my heart towards those who were richer, or brighter, or in any way better off than I; and they made me wretched. But now I mean to be contented, and to make all I can of myself just where God has placed me, and with just the talents he has given me, even if they are small and few. Don't you remember, grandfather used to say, 'Folks never could be on an equality in this life, —for God didn't make 'em alike, and didn't mean 'em to be alike'? I see it is so, and that some are designed to do one thing and some another, and that each may be happy in doing what he was meant to do. Now, Sydney can no more do the work on the farm that I did at his age, than I could have solved the problems in mathematics which he works out; but he can do better things. I don't envy him now. I mean to help him all I can to make the most of himself. He will be sure to make a first-rate scholar, and some day we shall all be very proud of him. Mother, don't you think so?"

"You are my good, noble-hearted boy," said the mother, tenderly: "I never shall be prouder of Sydney than I am of you, Leonard."

"Oh, yes, you will, when he stands up in the pulpit, or gets into Congress, or some other high position," said Leonard, laughing. "But we'll each be a comfort to you in our own way, mother, and we'll all help one another along the best we can. Here's Mabel will be sure to do her part,—' my *goodest* sister,' as Sydney used to call her before he could speak plain."

"I have been blessed in my children," said the mother, wiping her eyes; "I could not ask for better ones. But I don't want my youngest spoiled by being too much petted. He has never yet made sacrifices for others; for others have always done for him; and that is just the way to make him a selfish man, you know."

"But Sydney isn't a bit selfish," said Mabel, indignantly: "he's as warm-hearted a boy as ever was!"

"Yes, he's impulsive and generous by nature; but when you are as old as I am you will find that a great many boys of that temperament become selfish and exacting men,—that is, selfish in a certain way; always willing others should do for them, and expecting they will. So far, Sydney has been the petted one of our family; and I think he ought now to exert himself more. He might do something to pay for his board, at least. I don't want you to be overworking yourself and going without things you really need, to help him.. It isn't right, and it's no real kindness to him to carry him over all the hard places."

So spoke the sensible, experienced mother; but, when she had retired for the night, the good brother and loving sister sat up planning how they might make sacrifices for their favourite. It was easier for them to make them than not to make them; and as for Sydney, when he was older and had finished his education, they said, he would be sure to do a great deal more for them than they ever had done for him.

"I think mother is too hard on Sydney," said Mabel. "He's only just young and thoughtless. If he knew we put ourselves out for him, it would make him unhappy. Now, I really do not need a new shawl or dress the least bit in the world, and——"

"And I can do well enough without a new suit in the fall," said Leonard.

"Oh, Leonard! your freedom-suit! You must have that!"

"No, not if Sydney is kept at school through the year. He can't work for his board; it isn't in him to work: it's in him to study, and nothing else."

So, after divers talks and consultations, it was decided by the time Sydney came home for his vacation that he should return to school; and the light-hearted, bright-eyed youth rejoiced in the fact, without any just idea of what it cost. It is always so in this life: the self-sacrificing ones continue to make sacrifices, reaping a rich reward in the joy of their own hearts for doing so; while the genius of

## AN OFFENSIVE CHARACTER. 173

the family continues charmingly oblivious of the fact. We are not complaining of this. Some, by the very necessity of their nature, must work for others, and are only happy while doing it; while others seem to need perpetual sunshine to develop their capacities, and, unless they are carefully sheltered from exposure and hardship in their youth, can never become the blessings to the world they were designed to be. Only let the latter never forget that, if the toil of manual labour is not required of all, all are bound to respect those who do labour, and to render an equivalent to the world in service of a different kind; and let them carefully guard themselves against becoming exacting and selfish, as well as against any feeling of superiority. If there is a being in the world whom it is difficult to regard with complacency, it is he who, lifted up to a higher position in life by the sacrifices and toils of the humbler members of his family, fancies himself their superior, and either forgets their existence altogether or condescendingly patronizes them as his inferiors.

Such a sad requital for their loving labours, it is to be hoped, was not in store for Leonard and Mabel Roberts. At present the young scholar was certainly as modest and affectionate a brother as they could wish. He was still shy in his intercourse with strangers, only kindling into brilliancy when perfectly at his ease by the kitchen-fireside of the old red house, or in the school-room, where he stood the acknowledged superior in all his classes.

## CHAPTER XIII.

### THE WOOD-LOT.

It was now March; but there was still snow lying on the ground, and the sleighing on the highlands of Woodlee continued good. The morning after the little debate on Sydney's future, Leonard and Mabel were, as usual, both astir before the first streak of dawn. He had his horses, cows and sheep to feed and look after, and the cows to milk; and she must prepare the early breakfast.

"Where are you going to-day?" asked his mother, who joined them at the breakfast-table.

"Over to the wood-lot, to draw some more wood to the judge," said Leonard.

"I thought you were through with sledding for this year."

"I thought so too; but he was very anxious I should get him five cords more, and offered a good price for it: so I've promised to draw it if the sleighing holds on a little longer."

The breakfast of beef-steak and baked potatoes was eaten. They always had a warm meat-breakfast when Leonard went to the wood-lot, for he did not come home to eat again till his day's work was over. A chapter from God's holy word was reverently read, and the morning prayer for his blessing offered; and when Leonard drove out through the gate, the sun was only just looking over the East-hill ridge. It was a cold, blustering morning, but he whistled a lively tune as he jumped on his sled, for the blood in his veins circulated far too briskly for any March wind to chill it, and his heart was light and buoyant with a thousand hopes.

It had been a hard winter's work to clear that lot on the side-hill from its heavy growth of timber, and Leonard had worked there steadily for months,—" worked like a *dog*," John Hall said,—like a high-spirited, brave-hearted, energetic *man*, we should say,—and, by the help of one hired hand, he had done wonders. The grand old forest-trees, whose heads had been uplifted for many a year towards the sky in sunshine and in storm, had been levelled to the ground. Such of them as were suitable for building-purposes had been hauled to the saw-mill, and the rest drawn to the village for fire-wood or piled up in long rows by the side of the road for sale. In order to do this, they had often waded about in deep drifts above their knees, for it had been a severe winter; but Leonard was never cold, and always laughed heartily when his mother, who felt chilly sitting by the fire, worried about his exposing himself so much. He was usually tired—often extremely tired—when he got home; but it was a wholesome fatigue, insuring a good night's sleep. Indeed, he was seldom too tired to go to the evening singing-school if there was one in the village, and to walk home half a mile in an opposite direction with Susan Lee, who had now risen up into a well-grown, rosy-cheeked maiden of eighteen.

Neither was he often too tired to read aloud from the book of travels or history which Mabel had taken from the library. It had been a habit of his father's to read aloud in the winter-evenings, and his mother had trained Leonard to do the same, while she and his sisters sewed. Now she sat in her rocking-chair in the corner and knit, while Mabel sewed by the little table, and Leonard drew up to the other side of it with his book. He did not read particularly well, for he was by no means a finished scholar; but they could understand, and so did he, and in this way he was becoming an intelligent young man, who knew something about the world he lived in, and its inhabitants, and whose views of things in general were becoming enlarged and liberal. He read slowly, and he took in an idea slowly; but when it was taken in, he retained it: he pondered on it, and made it his own. No, Leonard was not brilliant nor quick. He was just a plain, sensible, hard-working young farmer, such as the poorest New England lad may become; but he was the comfort of his mother's heart,—her *home-boy*, her protector and support.

On this windy morning, as he drove along, cheerily facing the blast, his heart was full of bright hopes of the future; for he felt within himself not only a consciousness of power to wrestle with the hardships that lay before him, but also to overcome them. He was no coward to sit down and repine because the way was hard and the conflict sharp; but he was brave-hearted and strong-bodied, and he meant to meet the toils and trials of his lot as a brave man should. He had a young man's health, a young man's hopefulness, and, more than all, he was conscious of an honesty of purpose which enabled him to look upward fearlessly for a blessing on his plans. Honest both towards God and towards man, what had he to fear? There was no dark place in his heart to be covered up, no miserable foreboding of detection or coming retribution lurking there; but instead of these there were peace and light in his whole soul; and his countenance and bearing were open, straightforward and manly, as became an honest, true-hearted working-man.

As he glanced over the cleared space, now looking bare and desolate, he saw in imagination a beautiful crop of wheat waving there; and when he thought of the money that wheat would bring in market, he rejoiced, not with a sordid delight in mere accumulation, but because he could do so many good and desirable things with it, for his mother, for Sydney and for Mabel. For himself, too, he had cherished plans lying hidden away in the warmest corner of his heart: what young man has not? But they were good, pure, upright plans, such as he need not blush to own to God or man.

With a hand made dexterous and strong by use, he quickly loaded his sled, carefully measured his load, and set off with it in the direction of the village. As he was driving by Dr. Willard's door, some one hailed him.

"What will you take, Roberts, for that load of wood?" inquired the doctor.

"It's engaged, sir."

"Have you any more like it?"

"Only two or three cords. I have a plenty of wood, but it isn't so straight and sound as this."

"What do you ask a cord?"

"Judge Bailey gives me three dollars and a half."

"That is a great price,—more than men in general ask."

"Yes, sir; but it's an uncommonly good lot of wood."

"Could you bring me three cords this week?"

"Not this week. I've engaged all I can draw for several days."

The doctor hesitated. "I'm in want of some immediately."

At this juncture, another load from the opposite direction came up the road, and Leonard drove on. The driver of the other load was Jim Barker, an old schoolmate of Leonard's.

"Want a load of wood, doctor?" he asked.

"Yes, if you've got a good one."

"First-rate, doctor,—good hard maple and oak, every stick on't."

The doctor looked at it carefully. It looked well on the outside, and, after some chaffering about the price,—for Jim, hearing Leonard say he was to have three dollars and a half, raised the price on his,—he concluded to take it, and it was driven into the yard.

When Leonard drove his load through the gate at Judge Bailey's, the judge himself came out to look at it.

"You are punctual, I see," he said. "It is a real pleasure to deal with a man who does a thing when he says he will."

Leonard smiled. He always made an effort to keep an engagement, considering it as something binding and sacred.

"I've brought you a capital load, sir," he said. "There isn't a crooked stick in it."

"It looks well. How much is there?" asked the judge.

"A cord and a quarter, plump. You'll find it will hold out, I think."

"I am willing to take your word for it, Leonard; and that is what I would not do by any other wood-seller in town."

"I'd rather you would measure it yourself, sir," said Leonard, blushing with pleasure. "I meant to measure it carefully, but there may be some mistake. It's always expected the purchaser will measure it."

"I know it is, and there is generally need enough of it; but, Leonard, you've brought me wood ever since you were a boy of sixteen, and I never knew a load fall short, or prove different from what you told me. Your loads are never fair on the outside and filled up with trash. No, I am as willing to trust you as I am myself, to give me fair good measure."

Leonard's heart beat proudly at this tribute to his honesty; for Judge Bailey was still the great man of Woodlee.

"Thank you, sir," he said, modestly. "I was trained to be honest, and to never try to make a thing seem different from what it really is."

"I do not doubt that. I do not doubt it at all. It runs in the blood. A more honourable man than your grandfather, the old captain, never lived. He wouldn't on any account have wronged a man out of a single cent. Everybody knew just where to find him, and your father too. There never were two honester men than they; and I am glad you are going to keep up the family reputation. The truth is, I offered you half a dollar a cord more, because I knew your wood was a good deal better than I can buy of anybody else."

"That is being fair on your side too, sir," said Leonard. "There are some buyers who screw us down to the very lowest cent, and who won't pay any more for a good load than a poor one."

"I know it, and it is just a premium on dishonesty. I like a good article, and am willing to pay a good price for it."

"I wish it was so with all buyers," said Leonard : "it would make it much easier for us poor farmers who have to sell as we can."

"Both buyers and sellers need a higher-toned morality," said the judge. "It is a sad fact that each tries to overreach the other in their bargains; that is, the great majority do. There are some thoroughly honest men in all communities, I hope. But, Leonard, don't be calling yourself poor. You are a thriving, prosperous young fellow. The farm is looking up now; and you'll bring in a splendid piece of grain on that side-hill next year. I keep a little eye on your affairs; for I always like to see a young man working his way up by his own industry and integrity."

The load of wood was soon thrown off, and Leonard was on his way to the woodlot for a second, all the happier for this word of encouragement and approbation.

He was returning home at night, tired and hungry, and withal a little impatient; for he had been hindered more than usual during the day, and it was now dusk,— when Dr. Willard again called to him.

"I say, Roberts, can't you bring me three cords of wood this week?"

"Not this week. I have engaged all I can possibly draw this week."

"Early next week, then? I'm in great want of some."

"I can't promise, sir," said Leonard. "If the sleighing lasts, I might draw you some the last of the week." And he drove on, as the doctor made no reply, saying to himself, "I wonder he don't buy it of Jim Baker. He wants to sell."

If he had followed the doctor into his house, he would have found out the reason. The irritable little man was in a state of high exasperation. He had neglected to get a supply of wood at the proper time, and it was now getting short, and the weather was very cold.

"Confound these wood-sellers!" he exclaimed; "they are all a set of scamps."

"Not all, I hope," replied his meek little wife.

"That load I got this morning was a perfect shave! It looked well enough on the outside, but it was filled in with wretched trash,—not a stick of it bigger than my arm, and as crooked as a pothook. And then it was piled so that there wasn't more than three-quarters of a cord. It was a miserable cheat throughout. No, I don't believe there's an honest woodseller in the town! I've been cheated in every load I've bought this winter; sometimes in quantity, and sometimes in quality, and sometimes in both. They're a swindling set."

"The Baileys say young Roberts deals very fairly. Can't you get some of him?"

"No! there ain't the least accommodation about him. He won't bring a load only just when it suits his own convenience. But I won't buy another load of Baker, if I go without,—that's a settled thing!"

A few days later, Leonard drew him three cords of wood of so good a quality and so fairly piled, that even the fault-finding doctor was compelled to own he had been honestly dealt by.

"If there *is* an honest wood-seller in the place," he observed to his wife, after surveying it carefully, "I desire to deal with him in future. I am willing to pay a good price for a good article; and this young Roberts really seems to be a genuine, honest fellow. I told him I'd take all my wood of him another year."

Many who saw Leonard prospering, and by degrees becoming trusted and respected by the best citizens of the place, called him a lucky fellow; but his luck consisted merely in being industrious, punctual in fulfilling his engagements, and in always doing what was honourable in all his dealings with them,—a kind of *luck* every young man can share if he only chooses to.

## CHAPTER XIV.

#### THE BIRTHDAY.

During the following spring and summer, Leonard worked early and late; and he was repaid in autumn by the abundant harvests he gathered in. He was surprised at his own success; and when his grain, wool and cheese were sold, and all outstanding amounts paid, he felt justified in buying himself a nice suit of clothes to celebrate the advent of his majority, for at his next birthday he would be twenty-one. The barn had been shingled, some little additions made to the house, and Sydney kept in school through the summer, only spending the vacations at home. Leonard, in addition, could afford to make a little present to Mabel,—the faithful helper in all his toils,—something useful, of course; for in the red house nothing merely ornamental could be thought of,—at least not now,—nor till Sydney was able to support himself.

This led to many private consultations with his mother, in which it was decided that a merino dress was what she most needed, and that it should be a blue merino. But who could select it?—Who would be sure of finding the right texture and shade of colour? Not Leonard, with his rough, clumsy fingers; nor the mother, who seldom went from home, except to church. And a merino dress so nice and pretty as this must be, was not to be found in Woodlee, but must be bought in the county-town adjoining. What could be more natural than to ask Susan Lee, who went there frequently, to make the purchase?

This was probably the reason why Leonard called to see her several times, and walked home from singing-school with her more frequently than usual, having many little agreeable chats with her. It was by no means an easy thing to decide just what that blue merino dress should be!

Leonard's birthday was on the second of November, and his mother and Mabel planned to give a little party on that day. Eight or ten young girls of his own age were to be asked to a cosy tea-drinking, and an equal number of young men invited to join them in the evening; for such was the etiquette of Woodlee.

Leonard and Mabel, when the evening came, were both arrayed in their new apparel. His was a suit of dark-blue cloth, and, having on this great occasion indulged in the extravagance of having it cut by the best tailor in the county, it fitted him extremely well, and was very becoming to his bright, manly face and well-developed figure. He was a son any mother might be proud of, standing there with his frank, honest face, his strong arm, and his brave, true heart, which would never prove false to friend or foe. She was proud of him, and rejoiced in him; and, as she gazed at him with tender eyes, she felt a longing, almost acute enough to be painful, to have his father and grandfather there to see how good and noble he looked, how worthy to be their son and the master of the old red house.

Did they behold him? Were there unseen eyes gazing fondly on the boy they had once loved, and rejoicing in the bright promise of his manhood? Who can say? Who knows how thin the veil may be which hangs between us and the spiritual world and the beings who inhabit it?

And Mabel, the good sister, always thoughtful of others and unmindful of herself, her cheeks glowing with pleasurable excitement, watching to see that no one was neglected or uncomfortable, and never once thinking how becoming that soft shade of blue was to her fair cheek,— she, too, no less than Leonard, was the joy and pride of her mother's heart that night.

Leonard's old friend, John Hall, was there,—a tall, broad-shouldered youth, ready to help on with all the fun and frolic; Sydney was there too, standing by his mother's side,—slender, light-haired, with almost feminine delicacy of feature, a perfect contrast to Leonard in personal appearance. He looked very young, and peculiarly unfitted for any hardship; and one seeing him did not wonder that protecting arms were thrown around him, and that the stronger brother and sister so eagerly sought to shield him from all danger and exposure.

There was another old friend of our's also present,—Susan Lee. With her trim little figure, her black eyes flashing with mirth and mischief, and a colour on her cheeks which could only have been caught from the sunny side of the peaches in her father's garden, she was now blooming out into a very attractive maiden. She entered

## AN ERA.

with a keen relish into all the innocent gayeties of the evening; yet there was a certain shyness in her eye, a dropping of the lid, a warm suffusion of the cheek, when she met the gaze of the young hero of the hour. Perhaps no one noticed this but Mabel; but it awakened in her heart a train of new and anxious thought, which kept her waking long after the house was buried in silence and all eyes but her's sealed in sleep. But at length she was able to put aside the anxiety; and her true woman's heart, just even in its tenderness, recognized the fitness of that divine law which binds human hearts together in a union closer and more sacred than that even of brother and sister, mother and child.

To Leonard himself the day had not passed without many serious reflections. It was an era in his life. He had reached the Rubicon which separated youth from manhood, and must now face new duties and dangers. That night, after the enjoyment and excitement of the evening had passed away, he stood looking out of his chamber-window. It was a clear, frosty night, and the heavens were glowing with countless myriads of stars. What stirring thoughts came to him as he gazed,—what memories of his boyhood, when he sat by the door-stone and heard his grandfather talk of *his* young days and of Gilbert Watson's death-bed! It was a beautiful image he had in his mind of that dear old grandfather, with his snowy locks and placid features; and there now came distinctly to his recollection many wise things he had heard him say about life and its duties. What a different meaning the words had now, from what they had when he heard them with boyish ears! Yes, he was no longer a boy, but a man; and he pondered seriously that night what manhood meant, and in what consisted a man's prerogatives and privileges, a man's responsibilities and duties.

As we have said, Leonard did not shrink

from encountering the hardships of a poor man's life. Instead of this, he rather rejoiced that he had his own way to make. It would not have suited him to be a mere recipient,—to hold large possessions which he had done nothing towards earning. He looked forward hopefully into life; he meant to make it something good and noble, something rich and precious. Life was a gift from God, and he hoped not to waste or fritter it away, but to fill it with worthy deeds,—quiet, every-day home-deeds,—for Leonard was not imaginative, and never dreamed of doing brilliant or startling things,—but yet honourable, useful deeds, which would make his little world the better and happier for his living in it.

Those glittering stars, holding on their course so silently in the broad heavens, had been shining there just so serenely since he had watched them, when a child at his grandfather's knee, with a vague feeling of awe and admiration. They changed not; but his thoughts, his hopes, his life,—how these had changed since then! How they had all deepened and intensified! And the heart of the young man glowed within him as he looked upward; for the Creator of those worlds, Himself more serene, more unchanging, than they, was his God, his Father, the source of his life; the fountain from which flowed forth all the strength to will and to do which nerved his heart; the Being to whom he was indissolubly united, and for whose blessing and guidance he might hope in every step of the life before him.

So the new life of Leonard Roberts—his *man's* life—opened with fervent thanksgiving and earnest prayer, offered in the presence of those shining stars to their great Creator,—offered in faith and sincerity, and doubtless heard by Him who answereth prayer.

## CHAPTER XV.

### VOTING.

THE first town-meeting held in Woodlee after Leonard attained his majority was for the choice of a Governor and State Senators and Representatives. It is to be hoped that few young men exercise the elective franchise for the first time without some serious thought of their duties as freemen and citizens. To Leonard, with his early training and the counsels and warnings of his grandfather still fresh in his memory, it was an event of unusual interest. How well he remembered going to the town-meeting with his grandfather the last day of his life, and his telling him and John, "One of these days you'll have to make a serious business of this. See to it that you allers vote for the man who's honest and true to his country; for if you vote for bad men, your having a right to vote will be a curse, and not a blessing."

Leonard, now that the time had come, honestly wished to be a loyal citizen and a true patriot. He had, of course, no political influence. It was only his one vote to cast; but he knew that if every man looked well to his one vote, the right result would certainly be secured: so that it was important to cast that honestly and in the fear of God. It was the one talent given to him, and for which God held him responsible.

But one difficulty met him at the threshold. Each man could not vote for the person he individually considered the best man in the State for Governor or whatever office was to be filled: if he did, there would be as many different men voted for as there were voters, and endless confusion would ensue. Hence there must be some organization, some system. He found that such an organization did actually exist. There were two great parties, holding opinions widely different on matters of both State and national policy, and each of these had met together and selected a candidate who was supposed to represent the views of the party nominating him, and was expected to carry out these views if elected. For one or the other of these he must vote in order to have his vote of any avail. But what if neither of these candidates held such opinions or bore such a character as he could honestly approve? What would be his duty then? Not to vote at all, to vote by himself, or to vote for whichever of the two candidates he considered nearest right, though he might deem him wrong in some essential points? Fortunately, this was not a practical question at this election, for he had confidence, both politically and morally, in the nominees of one party; but he could not help feeling that at some time it might perplex him, and he laid it by for careful consideration. "I wish I had grandfather to go to now, as I had when I was a little boy," he said to himself. "I am sure he could answer this question for me." But he knew that wisdom and guidance from a still higher source were promised him, and that gave him confidence and strength.

"Two things a man in this country has to do," old Captain Roberts had said, long years before. "One is to vote; the other, to learn how to vote."

Leonard hoped he had learned how to vote; at least, he had tried to learn. He had informed himself as well as he could about the condition and government of his country, had carefully studied the Constitution of the United States and that of his own State,* and made himself to some degree familiar with the opinions of the prevailing political parties. History, especially the history of his own country, had

---

* In one of the States (perhaps in others) a school-book is in use which describes the leading duties of citizens and officers, and the general laws of the nation and State, in a simple and concise series of questions and answers. It seems very desirable that our young men so soon to be ruling citizens should become familiar with the national and State Constitutions.

been his favourite reading. He and John Hall had had warm disputes about the comparative merits of Hannibal and Scipio, and other generals of ancient times, as long ago as when they sat on the same bench at the public school and studied the History of Rome together; and in later years he had read attentively such works of history as he could procure, and also the speeches of our members of Congress and other prominent men. Of course, at his age his views were crude, and not so well balanced as they would be twenty years later; but he had decided opinions, and had formed them as honestly as he knew how. He believed one party was maintaining sound principles, such as God approved : so that his way was clear before him in this election at least; and he went to the polls in fine spirits, proud to be a voter, and proud of being an American citizen, with the rights and privileges of that position.

Going over to town, he fell in with his old crony, John Hall. Their early friendship still continued, though they were not exactly intimate now; for the two acted from different motives, and often took opposite views of things. It was so in politics, and it was well understood by both that they would vote different tickets.

"One thing I can tell you, Leonard," said John, after a little good-natured bantering: "your ticket won't be elected: you may be sure of that."

"Perhaps not," said Leonard; "but with that I have nothing to do. I shall do all I can to elect him whom I believe to be the best man; and that is all I have to do."

"I don't want to belong to the losing party all my life," said John.

"I hope *I* sha'n't," answered Leonard, laughing; "and I expect the right party will prevail another year, if it doesn't this. But if I knew it wouldn't, I should vote for it just the same."

"Your head always was full of notions, Leonard, and always will be, I suppose.

You'll never have any influence, with your impracticable ideas of right and wrong. We've got to take the world as it is, and accommodate ourselves to it. Now, I mean to make myself a position and be somebody. I don't intend to stay in this mean, out-of-the-way place. I've got as much talent as half the men who go to our large cities and get to be the smartest men there. If I stay on here and drudge, I shall never be of any account, that's certain."

"*I* never expect to do any thing but drudge, as you call it," said Leonard. "I expect to stay here all my life and work hard for a living; but I mean to respect myself, and to be respectable, for all that."

"I won't be a farmer," said John. "I never was made for that. I'll tell you, Leonard, what I am going to do,—though it isn't to be spoken of just yet. I've got an uncle at the South who is a lawyer: he will let me study law with him, and I am going down to him next fall. I can't afford to go through college; but you know Clay and a good many other great men never did that. I shall get a good start with Uncle William, and, once started, I can make my own way. I have got talent enough to get on. I feel sure of that."

"I dare say you have, John," said Leonard, sympathizingly. "You always could do what you had a mind to. But you don't like to work, John. That will be the trouble with you, I am afraid."

"But you will see I shall work when I get something to do that suits me. As you say, I could always do what I had a mind to; and I have a mind to make myself a distinguished lawyer, and I *shall!*"

Leonard wondered whether one who had never yet applied himself to any thing could, at twenty-one, turn over a new leaf and work perseveringly in a profession.

"Well, John," he said, "I trust you will succeed, and make good old Woodlee proud of you, some day. But when you are a great man I hope you will think more of what is for the good of the country than most great men do, and not merely look after your own interest."

"Oh, of course I shall. At first, I must think how to get on myself; but when I've got a position, then I can act independently and for the public good, you know."

John Hall was cherishing the delusive dream which has so often beguiled ambitious young men into acting from expediency at first. But whoever hopes to be an upright politician must begin his career by being upright as a man. Beginning with sacrificing principle, he will find it at every step more difficult to become straightforward; and should he gain place and power, he will be trammelled in a thousand ways he little dreamed of at first

Arrived at *the green*, as the little space around Woodlee church and town-hall was called,—for it had a town-hall now,—they found a crowd already there. As they came up, Judge Bailey, who was standing near the door, seeing Leonard, spoke to him.

"Going to vote to-day for the first time," said he, "and to vote in the right way, I hope? Shall I give you a ticket? I have some here." And he handed out a printed ballot.

Leonard had a great respect for Judge Bailey, as great as for any man in town; and, besides, he had received such kind treatment from him at all times, that he really would have liked to take the ticket. "Take it: if you do not use it, he'll never know it," said an insinuating voice within; but it was at once silenced by the better voice of conscience. Leonard felt that he might as well be outspoken, and have it understood on which side he should vote: so he said, respectfully, though colouring deeply,—

"I have decided to vote the other ticket, sir."

"You have! *Why*, I should like to know?" asked the judge, coolly.

Leonard was still more painfully embarrassed. He was never fluent, and was now much perplexed at being questioned by one so much his superior in years and station; but the voice within whispered, "Be true to yourself: no shirking nor equivocating!" So he said, hesitatingly,—

"Because I think they uphold right principles, sir."

"And it is easy at twenty-one to know exactly what right principles are!" said the judge, sarcastically. "A few years hence, when you are a little wiser, you won't, perhaps, find it quite so easy."

"I'll take that ticket, if you please, judge," said John, willing to show the judge what side he had espoused.

"Your convictions, then, are different from Leonard's," said the judge, smiling. "I am glad to find you are going to start right." And the judge and John walked off together, the former thinking to himself, "Well, at twenty-one I believe I was just as confident and frank as young Roberts is." And he sighed, and half wished he was a boy again.

"Can it be that I am wrong?" thought Leonard, as he looked after them. "The judge is so much older and wiser than I, he ought to know." But he remembered that he had not made up his mind hastily, but deliberately and after asking to be guided. "I must abide by my convictions: it's the only fair and honest thing to do," he said to himself, as he went up the steps. He entered the hall, and as soon as the polls were open, he went up and quietly deposited his vote.

When he came out of the hall, there were, as usual, a good many standing about, discussing the news of the day or cracking jokes, while waiting for the votes to be counted. In one of these groups stood Colonel Towne, an old and influential citizen of Woodlee, who had been a good friend both to Leonard's father and grandfather. Seeing Leonard, he spoke to him, and congratulated him on having arrived at the honour of depositing his first vote.

"I don't know, for my part, whether it's

a thing to be glad of or not," said Deacon Whipple, another old inhabitant. "This voting is a dreadfully perplexing business, it's so hard to tell what's right and what's wrong now-a-days."

"It always was, I suspect," said the colonel, rather dryly.

"Why, no; things wa'n't so mixed up when we were young, colonel. Then there were the old Democrats and Federals, and they were as far apart as light and darkness; but now there are half a dozen parties, each with some right in't and some wrong, and all so tangled and mixed up together, a man don't know what's what, without he's got sharper wits than I have."

"But there is a right and there is a wrong," said the colonel; "and I believe if a man honestly tries to find the right, he can,—in politics as well as in other things."

"You go for 'the higher law,' as they say, then, colonel?"

"Certainly I do. Every Christian citizen

must. Demagogues and mere party men may sneer at the phrase, but every man's conscience tells him that all questions should be brought to this one standard:—Is it right or wrong in the sight of God?"

"But we are to be governed by human laws in political affairs."

"That is true; but I do not believe that God is therefore to be left out of the account. It is because I believe the laws of our land are based on God's laws, and in accordance with law, that I yield a hearty allegiance to them. I don't think they are perfect; but, if ever public men were guided from above, I think those were who founded our government; and therefore I believe they laid its foundations deep and strong enough to resist all the commotions that agitate the community. These party distinctions you speak of, deacon, are chiefly about local and temporary matters, and will pass away as others have done; and in a few years people will wonder they were ever so much excited over them, while underneath the tumult lie the foundations of law and order, still firm and unchangeable.

"Yes," he added, seeing Leonard was listening to the conversation, "the thing I would most earnestly impress on a young man who is just commencing his political life, as our young friend here is, is this:— Always uphold what you believe to be right in the sight of God, in politics. Serve him in this as well as in other things."

"A man won't make much headway in the world if he sticks to such notions as those, I reckon," said Jim Baker, who had joined the group.

"Perhaps he won't get into office, if that is what you mean," said the colonel, with some severity in his tone. "And yet I believe in my very soul—and I've had some experience in public matters—that the highest right is the highest expediency; in other words, that doing right is the surest way to success, in any true meaning of the term. Let a man be thoroughly upright, and in time he will gain the confidence of the community; they know where to find him; while one who has no conscience, but merely wants to be popular and get the most votes, however he may succeed and be admired and followed for a time, is pretty sure to be sooner or later understood and despised. How many men we have seen in office of this stamp, who rode on the top wave of popular applause for a few months or years, and where are they now?"

"But, after all," said the deacon, "there's a good many don't want a man to be too honest. They'll vote the quicker for one who goes for his party right or wrong, without too many conscientious scruples."

"Yes, there are a great many such voters, no doubt," replied the colonel,— "far too many; but I do hope we are not yet sunk so low that they constitute the majority in our country. I have faith in the people yet, and that they are capable of governing themselves. I had rather trust the government to them, at any rate, than to any one man or any set of men, such as rule in most other countries. But to do this," he said, earnestly, "our people must be kept intelligent and virtuous. That is what the safety of our nation depends on,—the honesty and virtue of the people,—the common people!"

"Just what grandfather used to say," thought Leonard, as he walked away. And, he thought, perhaps when he was perplexed he should venture to go to the good colonel for advice.

## CHAPTER XVI.

### EIGHTEEN HUNDRED AND SIXTY.

WE pass over another term of years, and then look in again on our old friends in the red house. Leonard Roberts is now thirty years of age,—a quiet, thoughtful, and rather grave man,—seeming, as he always has seemed, a little older than his years; not in looks, for he is in the very perfection of manly vigour, hale, hearty and intensely active; but in character and purpose. We saw him when a boy, preparing for manhood by patiently enduring hardships and by being loyal to truth and duty; we saw him when a young man, still loyal to God and the right. We are now to look at him as a man in the prime of life, and find what fruits these preparatory years have ripened into maturity.

The red house,—there it stands on the brow of the hill, just the same modest, snug, unpretending little dwelling it always was, sheltered by the same chestnut-trees, now grown large and venerable. It is very little changed in any respect. But across the road there is to be seen another house, which is altogether a new feature in the landscape. That is a cottage also; but it is larger and more modern-looking, with piazzas about it, and is painted white, with green venetian blinds. In that we shall find Leonard Roberts established; and there, too, is Susan Lee,—no longer the young girl, but a faithful wife and mother. "How little she is changed!" we say, at first; but yet when we watch her going about her household duties with a quick step and careful eye, caressing or correcting the children, or welcoming her husband home with bright smiles, we feel that, though the same, she is not the same. That change from the young maiden to the matron modifies her face, movements and expression; but the change well becomes her; and she is more pleasing, now that her overflowing spirits are toned down a little. Yet she is still a contrast to her husband. If he is grave, she is sprightly. If he is reserved and slow to express his thoughts, she is mercurial and talkative. If he looks cautiously into the future, providing against emergencies, she makes the most of to-day, brightening every moment by her never-failing flow of spirits. Yet these differing traits do not produce a discord, but rather a harmony; and few homes are neater, sunnier or happier than this of Leonard Roberts.

Of course, where there are three children there are plenty of irritations and trials. Of course there are sleepless nights and wearisome days, and whole weeks when the burdens of life seem to press very heavily. Of course sickness comes, and disappointments and losses of different kinds; but in the midst of all, the hearty desire to do God's will and to be just and kind to one another operates like a charm—nay, far better than any magic charm—in spreading a genial and healthful atmosphere through all the house, calming, elevating and strengthening every inmate. When sorrows press heaviest, there is often found in that home a sweet peace and resignation almost better than joy; and when the clouds are lifted, there come gratitude and thanksgiving to the good Father who has never forsaken them in the darkest hour.

The oldest child is named after the dear old grandfather, Thomas,—Tom they call him: he is now a sturdy little fellow of seven, wide awake, and rather boisterous, save when his father's eye is on him; Lucy is fair and lovely, with all kinds of winsome ways; and the baby, Charlie, as yet like nothing in particular, except that he holds the whole house tributary to his slightest wish. How odd all this seems! for to us it appears but a little while since Leonard was a little fellow himself, trudging down the hill to school, and meeting Susan Lee at the corner of the lane.

It is easy to see that Leonard has prospered in his business. Every thing on the premises, house, barns, sheds, fences, show the presence of a thrifty manager. Indeed, he is considered the model farmer of the county. He has put up commodious buildings, bought back all the land which originally belonged to the farm, and added to it a broad strip of meadow. He has converted woodlands into grain-fields; and this golden month of October, 1860, finds him free from debt, and gathering in abundant harvests. Yes, a steady, upright, well-to-do farmer is Leonard Roberts,—a man universally respected and looked up to; and he has attained this position by being simply honest, industrious and frugal, and quietly doing his duty day by day.

If we step into the red house, we shall find young children there too. Whose can they be? Not Mabel's; for we feel sure, as we look at her quiet face, that she has always stayed at home. Not Sydney's; for he too is still unmarried. No: they are Lucy's two motherless little ones. We have said the passing years had brought trials. Perhaps one of the heaviest was when the news reached the red house that Lucy was dangerously ill, and destitute of the comforts and even the necessaries of life, in her Western home. Her husband had proved an intemperate man; and in a new country, among strangers, Lucy's once light, proud heart had been wellnigh broken by neglect and hardship. With a true wife's desire to shield her husband, she had concealed all his faults from her home-friends; and it was only through others they at last heard of her condition. After anxious consultation, it was decided that Leonard should go to Wisconsin and bring her home if it seemed best, or, in any event, do whatever he could for her relief.

But he returned without her. Alas!

before his arrival she had gone where no voice of friendship could reach her more! Her husband had sunk into a mere brute; and, waiting only long enough to see her decently interred, Leonard retraced his steps, bringing with him the two little children she had left. One of them was scarcely more than an infant; but he managed to get them home, and to lay them safely in his mother's arms.

"There is no one but us to care for them," he said, "and I knew you would be glad to have them with us, mother. They are all that is left of Lucy now,— our dear, light-hearted Lucy!"

Yes, the mother was glad to have them with her; and it was settled they should stay with her and Mabel; but the real burden of maintaining them must fall on Leonard. This he had foreseen; but during that night spent on the Western prairie, amid the desolation of Lucy's home, he had decided that it was right for him to do it. Some in his situation would have said they were heavily burdened already with a wife, mother, sister, and three children to maintain; but Leonard did not say this. If it was a right thing to do, then he must do it and take the consequences. He had that practical faith in God's promises that made him fearless where manifest duty was concerned, and always sure that what *ought* to be done *could* be done.

"Thank God," he had said to himself that night, "I have a wife whom I can trust. I know Susan will be even more willing than I to do what is right, and to make all the sacrifices that must be made." And he blessed her in his heart, while a thousand miles away from her on that lonely prairie, with a depth of love and tenderness he had never dreamed of when he first won her to be his bride.

Yes, Susan could be trusted. She must now go without the new furniture they had meant to buy for the pretty cottage, and without expensive clothing, and must economize in every way; but she did it cheerfully; for she too was a genuine, practical Christian, seeking first to know the will of her heavenly Father in all things, and then doing it patiently.

So Mabel and her mother went on taking the best of care of the puny children, while Leonard worked the harder and Susan economized the closer, and, if possible, smiled the brighter; and soon the little orphans thrived like flowers in May, and brought a world of bright sunshine into the red house.

"I do think they brought a blessing with them,—the dear little things," said Aunt Mabel. "To be sure, they are a deal of care and trouble; but I have never seen mother so happy since father died as she is now; and *I* wouldn't give them up for any thing,—the darlings!"

Yes, right-doing always does bring a blessing with it. God tells us over and over that it shall; but we strangely forget his words, and when we find he keeps his promises we are surprised, as if it was not a thing at all to be expected, and as if some strange event had happened to us.

Of all the inmates of the red house, Sydney had changed the most in these nine years. After fitting himself to teach, he went South as a private tutor in a family for three years, and on his return had entered college, and, by teaching part of his time, had slowly worked his way up, till he was now a member of the senior class. He was still a marked scholar, and as upright and conscientious perhaps as Leonard. But he had nothing of his brother's robust manliness. He shrank instinctively from opposition or ridicule, and, indeed, was morbidly sensitive on many points. Perhaps, however, he had more of the martyr in him than Leonard; for he suffered the very crucifixion of the flesh and spirit where Leonard would have scarcely suffered at all. He was still physically delicate, though not ill,—still had the sandy hair, light-blue eyes and delicate features of his childhood; but he was tall, and, when excited, his plain features would light up into an expression which showed how brightly within burned the concealed fires. He was a son and brother to be proud of and anxious about; and just now the great question of a profession was under consideration. His mother earnestly wished him to be a minister; but he shrank from committing himself to that profession, fearing he was not fit for it,—not thoroughly enough consecrated, body and soul, to the service of Christ. He had united with a church; but his ideal of an ambassador of Christ was so lofty and pure, and his searchings of his own heart so deep and thorough, that when the subject was pressed upon his notice for decision he was always greatly distressed, and begged to postpone it at least for a little longer.

As a compensation for his want of hopefulness, he had an ardent love for study, and an enthusiasm for all that was lovely in nature and intellect, which brought into his soul floods of joy which a nature less sensitive could never appreciate nor understand. The two brothers loved each other tenderly, and admired each other, each valuing in the other the qualities he himself lacked. When Sydney came home, they all enjoyed him thoroughly; for he took them into new regions of thought, and coloured whatever subject he touched with the hues of his own luxuriant fancy. He had inherited his mother's fervid temperament; for, as we said long ago, a latent vein of poetry was lurking in Mary Roberts's nature, and, prosy and humble as her life had been, it lurked there still. And, though now over sixty years of age, she entered into all Sydney's hopes and plans, and understood him as no one else in the family did. This peculiar sympathy between them was often very touching and beautiful, though it gave her many an anxious hour; and the question, "What can Sydney do in the world?" in spite of his rich gifts, usually brought a deep sigh with it from the mother's heart.

Thus we find our old friends in the red house in the autumn of 1860, that period so full of interest to the country, and of events which cast before them such dark and lengthening shadows.

## CHAPTER XVII.

### THE GREAT QUESTION.

OF the great public events which thronged thickly upon the close of that year, no intelligent citizen, like Leonard Roberts, could be an indifferent spectator. It was a winter of almost unparalleled severity in New England; but, fearfully as the snow-drifts were piled up around the cottages of Woodlee, the daily paper, with its exciting contents, found its way into many of them.

When the news came that State after State had seceded from this Union, declaring its right to do so and its reasons for it, Leonard read the ordinances issued by each carefully, considering candidly the causes assigned by them for their course. To him, as to most of the quiet citizens of the Northern States, the idea of a dissolution of the Union was new and startling. Politicians at the South had threatened it, and a few extremists at the North suggested it; but the great body of the people of the North had never once seriously thought of it as possible. Now they were compelled to look at it. Leonard Roberts was not a man to form an opinion hastily or from one point of view alone. On this, as on all other important subjects, he endeavoured to ascertain deliberately what truth and justice demanded, and to have his decision conformed to their requirements.

The question which at that juncture was the prominent one in all minds was this:— Is secession right? Can one of these United States lawfully separate herself from the great family of States? In order to answer this intelligently, Leonard Roberts again reviewed the Constitution of the United States, already familiar to him, but now studying each clause with special reference to this one question. He went anew over the history of its formation, and the history of the old Confederation, and read many of the able and exciting debates in Congress at that period, in order to ascertain from their own words what were the views of the framers of the Constitution on this vital point. What his conclusions were may be learned from a conversation which took place one evening, when the family were, as usual, all assembled to hear the daily paper read aloud. Sydney was at home for his vacation; and Mr. Price, a brother of Mrs. Roberts, was also making them a visit at the time.

"Well, Leonard," Mr. Price said, "what do you think of this new doctrine of secession? Do you believe a State has a right to go out of the Union in this way?"

"It is a great question, uncle," answered Leonard, "and one which I have been trying to answer honestly in my own mind. It is too important a one to be decided from impulse, or self-interest, or preconceived opinions; for it is a question involving life or death to our national institutions. I have tried to look at the whole subject candidly, and I must confess I can find no evidence of any right to secede. I don't believe the Constitution gives, or was meant to give, any such right. On the contrary, I think the great object the framers of it had in view was to do just what they themselves say in the preamble, —viz.: '*form a more perfect union.*' Now, for them to have given to each or any State a right to withdraw whenever it should choose to, would have undermined the very foundations of that union they were trying to establish more firmly; for with such a right there never could be, in the nature of things, any security or permanency to a union of States."

"So I think," said Mr. Price, who was called "Uncle Roger" at the red house. "Why, if every State, whenever it got angry or fancied itself abused, could go out of the Union any minute, who would know what to expect? Georgia might go out one year, New York the next, and then Illinois; and where would the nation be then?"

"True: there could be no security for any thing," said Leonard. "No foreign nation could feel confidence in a government based on such shifting sands. Neither our commerce nor any other great national interest could prosper on such uncertainties. Indeed, our own people couldn't feel any confidence in the government; for who could know what changes one year might bring? Now, I believe the men who framed the Constitution saw this clearly. They had tried the old Confederation, and found it fail in just that one point,—in not binding the States together firmly enough; and they meant to give us, in its place, a Union that should be strong and lasting. They did give us one which has hitherto proved so, and under which we have prospered wonderfully. Now its stability is to be subjected to a new test. If it stands this, we shall have a national government secured to us for all coming generations, resting on a firm basis, and shown to be strong enough to maintain itself against internal treachery as well as foreign foes. And I trust in God it may not be found wanting in this its day of trial! Don't you remember, mother," he added, after a little silence, "how grandfather used to charge us to stand by the old flag? I don't know but the time is coming when we shall have to rally under it on the battle-field, as our fathers did before us."

"God forbid!" exclaimed Mrs. Roberts, with a shudder. "War is such a dreadful thing that I hope I may never live to see another one,—especially a war among ourselves."

"A dreadful thing indeed it would be, mother," said Sydney; "but, dreadful as war is, there are still worse things. To betray one's country is worse. To stand still and see the nation rent asunder by wicked men is worse. To prove false to all our obligations as citizens, by letting the government purchased for us by our fathers be destroyed, without making a single effort to preserve it, would be worse. To have established in our land, which they meant should be a land of freedom, a nation openly based on slavery, would be worse. This would be treachery, falsehood, cowardice, disgrace,—worse, yes, a thousand times worse, than war! No man," he added, with flashing eyes, "who has one single drop of the old Revolutionary blood in his veins can look on and see these things attempted without doing what he can to stop it: if he does, he is false to every trust he holds as a citizen and a Christian,—false alike to his country and his God!"

"Yet war is such a terrible evil," said Leonard, more coolly, "that every thing which can be done, consistently with honour and duty, to prevent it ought to be done. I trust we shall yet escape it; for a civil war would be full of untold horrors. I fully believe, however, that God has given us this country as a precious inheritance for us to transmit to our children after us, an undivided and a free country, and that to thus hold it and transmit it is a solemn duty binding on every citizen of these United States. If an attempt is made to divide this country by force, then we must resist that attempt by force. It *must* be our duty to do this. I can come to no other conclusion. But I can't believe that even the hot-blooded Southerners will be insane enough to attempt this."

"*I* believe they will," said Sydney; "for when I was at the South I heard a dissolution of the Union so often talked about and threatened, that I think their minds are prepared for it. They expect foreign nations will come to their aid, and that they shall succeed in building up a great slaveholding, cotton-raising confederacy that will become immensely rich and powerful. This is the ambitious dream of their leading politicians; and I fear they will stop at nothing in trying to make it a reality."

"But why not let them go, if they want to?" asked Mabel. "For my part, I am sure I should rather live in a smaller and poorer country, if it were only free and quiet and governed by good laws."

"The question is not what we had rather do," said Leonard, "but what we ought to do. It would, no doubt, be easier and pleasanter for this generation to keep quiet and submit to all kinds of aggression and wrong, or even to let the country be divided at the instigation of wicked men, than to oppose it; but have we a right to do this? Our government and our country, with all the blessings belonging to them, were left to us; and are we not bound to do something to preserve them for those who shall come after us? If the people of the South, or rather the politicians of the South,—for I do not consider this so much a movement of the people as of their leaders,—have determined to strike a blow which will subvert the very foundations of our national existence, ought we to sit idle and let them do it? If secession meant merely dividing the country once,—though that would be bad enough,—it might possibly be endured; but don't you see, Mabel, that it is not merely the doing that, but the principle involved in it, which we are bound to resist? To introduce this precedent of the right of a State or States to secede at their pleasure, is to introduce a feature which will certainly prove our ruin; for, once admitted as a right which each State can claim, the door would be opened to its being done again at some future day, and then again, and so on indefinitely, till our nationality would be utterly gone. Allow this right, and we should have only a semblance of a government left; all its power and efficiency would be lost."

"We should then be pretty much in the same condition as the South American

States," said Uncle Roger,—"each separate State weak and unable to defend itself, and without any central government to maintain law and order over the whole."

"Yes, we should, indeed," said Leonard. "It is this bond of union which secures to us all our rights; and it must be the duty of every citizen to defend it, —yes, even if doing so costs us as much as it cost our fathers to establish it at first! No, Mabel, dearly as we love peace, we cannot let the government which secures such blessings to every citizen be destroyed, even if a war in its defence is the alternative; and we see that secession is but another name for destruction: ruin is as sure to come from it as effect is to follow cause,—not immediately, perhaps, not in our day, possibly, but eventually. So, if we love our government, if we love law and order and cherish the free institutions which have made us a great and happy people, we must resist this movement even to blood, if that alternative is forced upon us. We must settle it, once for all, that no State has a constitutional right to leave the Union when she chooses. Her people may, to be sure, exercise the right of revolution, common to all communities, if they see fit; but that is a different thing from claiming a right to secede from our Union."

"Another consideration," said Sydney, "makes it clear to me that we ought to resist it; and that is, the reasons which are given to justify secession. If we should allow that a State could ever leave the Union, we couldn't believe she was justified in doing it on any such pretext as is urged now; for if our present President hadn't been elected, I suppose they would have stayed in the Union."

"If they had elected their own Presidential candidate, they would probably have remained at least for a time. But the President was fairly elected; and what was their objection to him? Simply that he was opposed to the extension of slavery. It was not that he wished to interfere with it in the States where it already existed, and where it was generally admitted that the general government had no right to interfere. But he was pledged to resist its going into the vast common territory which belongs to the whole nation, and over which the national government has jurisdiction. Whatever minor causes of complaint existed, there cannot be a doubt that this was the main objection to his election."

"Yes," exclaimed Sydney, "here is the real antagonism between North and South. For this—the *extension* of slavery—the South is willing to divide the Union, and bring on a civil war and all the horrors which must attend it. For this she has attempted to leave the Union, and now resists the laws when our government tries to enforce them within her limits. Yes, it is clear to my mind that if secession ever could be justified in the sight of God,

it could not be on such a ground as this,—
to secure the extension of slavery!"

"But I don't see that we had interfered
even with their slavery," said Uncle Roger.

"No; the government certainly had
not," said Leonard; "for, however strong
a sentiment had existed against slavery
at the North, the government, for many
years, has been administered by those who
were in sympathy with Southern and not
with Northern feeling; and it would have
seemed only a dictate of decency to have
waited to see whether it was to be unconstitutionally interfered with by the
new Administration, before they withdrew
themselves. No, I cannot conceive a more
unjustifiable course than their's, look at it
in what light we will! And when we think
what slavery is," he added, "how contrary
to the spirit of Christianity, how blighting in its effects on both master and slave
and also on the community in which it
exists, how subversive of the best interests of humanity and civilization, I

have no words to express my abhorrence of that policy which would fasten it on vast regions now uninfected with it. There cannot be a doubt, in my mind, that in opposing its extension we are doing what the interests of humanity and the law of God alike require of us."

"These are tremendous issues to be met by any people," said Sydney.

"Yes, they are indeed. But if they must be met by this generation," replied Leonard, solemnly, "I pray God that we may be found worthy of such a responsibility,—worthy of the hour, and worthy of being the sons of our revolutionary fathers, who perilled every thing to secure a righteous and free government for their descendants."

"You and I, Leonard, are bound to be true to the flag of our Union and to the principles expressed by it," said Sydney, "let who will prove false to them. Why, I don't believe grandfather would sleep quietly in his grave if one of his descendants were to see that flag dishonoured without attempting to avenge the insult!"

"No, indeed," said Leonard; "for next to his God he loved and reverenced that. I can never forget how he used to look at it and talk about it."

"Oh, what would he have felt if he had lived to see it fired on by a traitor!" exclaimed Sydney. "If it had been a foreign foe, then we could have borne it; but that men reared under it and all their lives long protected and blessed by it should fire upon it, is more than I can understand. I should expect my hand to fall palsied while doing such a parricidal deed!"

"Yes, you and I will rally round the stars and stripes, Sydney, let what will come," said Leonard, "not alone for our fathers' sake, but for truth's sake, for freedom's sake, and because God requires it. There is where all true patriotism must be based. *First loyal to God, then loyal*

## A RESOLVE.

*to our country:*—that is my motto. I thank God that I can honestly feel that the North is right in this great contest,—that we are in favour of freedom as opposed to slavery, of law and order as opposed to confusion and anarchy, of justice and mercy as opposed to wrong and cruelty!"

"No," he added, after a moment's pause, looking at his little boy who lay sleeping on his mother's bosom, "I could not ask God's blessing on my children with a clear conscience unless I was willing to do all I could to leave my boys a country,—a blessed, united country, such as my fathers left to me; and, God helping me," he said, solemnly, "I pledge myself to do it, at whatever sacrifice to life or property."

"Amen!" responded Sydney.

A deep silence followed. An unutterable emotion, a strong sense of exaltation and inward strength, seized on the hearts of wife, mother and sister. Not one of them wished the words unspoken,—the vow unmade!

Susan rose and drew closer to her husband with the baby in her arms; while he cast on her a look of ineffable trust that was beautiful to see,—on her, the true wife that had never failed him!

"You too come of the old Revolutionary stock, Susan," he said; "I know you will never keep me back from doing my duty to my country."

"No, never!" she said, steadily: yet the lips which uttered the words were pale and quivering.

"God make us worthy to be the daughters of the women of the Revolution!" was the prayer which went up silently from the heart of every woman in the room. It was the prayer going up in those days from thousands of trembling hearts over all the hill-sides and in all the valleys of our land.

"If it be possible, let this cup pass from us." Thus prayed brave Christian men before the throne of God in those hours of fearful suspense and waiting; "but if war must come,—if we are forced to choose between that and treason to our country,—strengthen us, holy Father! to meet the peril as brave men should, and to be loyal to the end to our country and to thee!"

## CHAPTER XVIII.

### LOYALTY.

LOYAL! that is the word which most fitly expressed the feeling awakened throughout the whole North in the spring of 1861. It was a word which had been little used among us hitherto. Indeed, foreigners had asserted that the feeling signified by it could never exist where there was no crowned head on which to expend it,—as if it were less easy or noble to be loyal to a high and holy principle than to a mere creature of flesh and blood. But it was the word which exactly denoted Leonard Roberts's state of mind. To his heart's core he was loyal to his country,—loyal to the great principles of justice and freedom on which its government was founded, loyal to its laws, obeying them in all integrity of purpose, and loyal to the rulers placed by the laws over it. Of course he would be true to the country now in the hour of peril, and willing to sacrifice every thing to save it, if possible, from being torn asunder and destroyed.

This sentiment of loyalty had not been the sudden growth of a day or a month. No such deep pervading sentiment could be born of a sudden impulse. It is true, as his old grandfather had said long years before, that whoever would be thoroughly loyal as a citizen in his manhood must begin by being loyal to his parents and to God in his youth. Leonard had been true to his convictions of duty when he was a boy, doing what he thought it was right to do, and refraining from what he considered wrong; and it was to be expected he would do what he thought was right now he was a man, for it had become the habit of his life. When, a barefooted little urchin at school, he gave up his place in the class rather than be guilty of deception, he was preparing himself for an honest man. When he decided, as he sat on the rock at twilight, to sacrifice a great pleasure rather than do wrong, he was fitting himself, by the help of God, to be loyal to duty and to God in all his after-life. And now, when the responsibilities of manhood had gathered about him, he could not be false to his obligations as a citizen. To do what he considered right in the sight of God had become, it might almost be said, a matter of course now, so long had right-doing been the ruling purpose of his life.

Therefore, if he believed—as we have seen he did—that this Union of States ought to be preserved, he could no more refrain from throwing his whole strength into the cause of the Union than he could have committed any other known sin; for, with him, to be neutral in a conflict between right and wrong was the same as being an accomplice in the wrong. He had come to his conclusions cautiously; but now he must act in accordance with his convictions, cost what it might.

And when tidings came that Fort Sumter had been attacked and compelled to surrender, and afterwards that Union soldiers, when passing quietly through Baltimore on their way to the defence of the Capital, had been fired upon and killed, his whole soul was roused within him.

It was on Saturday evening, the 20th of April, that this last intelligence reached him, just at sunset, when he had finished the labours of the day and of the week. Silently he went into the house and brought out the old flag,—the time-worn, battle-stained flag which had been so sacred to him and to his ancestors,—and, unfurling it on the old spot, he sat down under a tree and gazed upon it as it rose and fell on the breath of the twilight breeze,—gazed long and silently at its faded folds, and then up at the blue heavens above, till his heart swelled with such lofty aspirations and purposes as can only stir the heart of a true patriot when his country is in peril. He sat there motionless till the stars came out, and as he looked up to the firmament where they were shining out so brightly and beautifully, his heart rose in prayer.

Leonard Roberts had been for many years a man of prayer; but he had seldom prayed as he prayed that night. His whole soul was quickened into intense emotion; and he turned to God, who knew all things, for teaching and guidance in that great crisis. He consecrated himself afresh, body and soul, all that he had and all that he was, to the service of God, to be guided by him wherever he should lead, even if it should be away from home and wife and children to die on the field of battle. In such an emergency, a single life seemed a small thing to give; and he asked God to help him to die cheerfully for his country if it should be necessary and right. He prayed, too, that his wife and mother might be strengthened to do

God's will; but far more fervently than for any thing else he poured out his supplications for his country in this its hour of danger,—that the God of hosts would be its God, its defence and shield, its leader and protector, filling the hearts of its rulers with wisdom, and the hearts of its citizens with a lofty patriotism that should enable them to do their whole duty in this emergency, and that all, rulers and people, might become a righteous and God-fearing nation, even through the terrible baptism of war and bloodshed, if God had so ordained.

His heart was calmed by prayer; but when he turned to his quiet home beneath the sheltering trees, and thought what agony his absence and death would bring into it, he felt a shrinking. But it was only for a moment; for, tenderly as he loved his wife and children, he felt that his country was more to him even than they,—or, rather, that only in being true to his country could he be really true to them.

He was a tender husband and father; but, with his home and family clearly standing out before him, he said, firmly, "My country first, in such an hour as this!"

As he passed by the door-steps of the red house, where he used to sit by his grandfather's knee long, long ago, the old man's words rushed upon his memory with strange power. He seemed to hear him once more saying, "I hope nobody who has got a single drop of my blood in his veins will ever suffer that blessed old flag to be trampled on and disgraced." Again he seemed to be putting his boyish hand on the old man's knee in token that *he* never would. Again he heard him saying, "You *can* be a patriot, Leonard: God grant you always may be!" And he felt that, like Hannibal, he had been consecrated to his country's service at nine years of age. That flag had now been dishonoured, fired upon by traitors; and, to his excited mind, his grandfather's voice seemed calling on him out of the still heavens to avenge the insult; and again he looked upward, and pledged himself to the service of his country through weal and woe.

The next day was the Sabbath,—such a Sabbath as never before dawned on our land! The sun rose fair and bright that April morning; and the blue heavens above, and the smiling earth beneath, were as calm and lovely as though no call to arms were ringing through the land, stirring men's souls like the sound of a trumpet. The whole land was moved to its very centre. In some sections, men were hurrying to the Capital; in others, women were gathered in the churches to sew, though sobs and prayers mingled with their work; and even in Woodlee, that quiet nook among the hills, but one subject was on all lips, one thought in all hearts; and from the old church-spire a beautiful bright flag, hastily made by the young women the day before, streamed bravely out upon the morning breeze. As Leonard and his family came in sight of it, and saw its folds waving out on the still air, every heart thrilled with a new sense of its value and sacredness.

"God bless the old flag!" said Leonard, "and help us all to be true to it, come what may! Tom, my boy," said he, lifting the little fellow up to get a better view of it, "look at the stars and stripes; look at them well, and when you've grown to be a man, remember your father told you, as his father told him, always to stand by that flag. Never desert it, let what will come, but shed your last drop of blood, if necessary, in its defence! Never be a traitor, Tom; *never*, as you hope for a father's blessing, or the blessing of God upon your soul!"

It was seldom that the quiet, reserved father spoke so earnestly; but in those days the souls even of quiet men were stirred to their very depths, till even the most slow-spoken became eloquent.

"It seems but a day, mother," he said, turning to the back seat where his mother was sitting, "since grandfather gave me the same charge."

"I was just thinking of that," said his mother, "and of how little he dreamed of such times as these coming in your day."

"And yet I remember perfectly his telling us one Fourth of July that we boys might live to see that flag floating over battle-fields, and that the time might come when we should have to fight to *preserve* our liberties as bravely as our fathers did to *establish* them."

"I remember that," said Susan. "I was only a little child, but mother took me to the tea-party, and I can see now just how the old gentleman looked as he stood up there talking so earnestly, and pointing up to the flag that hung from the liberty-pole close by. Of course I didn't understand what it meant; but his looks and tones of voice made such an impression on me that I have never forgotten them."

"It seemed very absurd then to talk of a war in our day," said Mrs. Roberts.

"And yet grandfather seemed to have a kind of premonition of just such a time as this," said Leonard; "for he never failed to charge us boys to stand by the old flag. And oh, mother, may strength be given to us now to follow his teaching and example!"

A heavy sigh came from the mother's heart; but she did not speak.

The services of the church in Woodlee, as in most other churches of our land on that day, had direct reference to the condition of the country. The ardent young clergyman offered up fervent prayers for the country, its rulers and people, and in his sermon set forth the obligations and duties of an American citizen in times of national peril so eloquently, and so earnestly urged on his hearers a faithful fulfilment of them, that many a young man in his congregation felt a new spirit of patriotism and self-sacrifice awakened within him. The service closed by singing the hymn commencing,—

"My country, 'tis of thee,
Sweet land of liberty,"

when all rose to their feet as by a simultaneous impulse and joined in singing it, while great tears might be seen rolling down the toil-hardened cheeks of the oldest and most phlegmatic men there. The closing stanza,—

> "Our fathers' God! to thee,
> Author of liberty,
> To thee we sing:
> Long may our land be bright
> With freedom's holy light!
> Protect us by thy might,
> Great God, our King!"

was sung as few stanzas were ever sung before in that little church; for the feeling in every heart was too deep to be suppressed.

It was a Sunday never to be forgotten; and the congregation went to their homes among the rugged hills with hearts glowing with patriotic fervour, determined to meet the impending crisis like brave, true-hearted men and women,—in fact, in very much the same frame of mind, we suppose, as did the congregations of New England in '75 and '76, when the prayers and exhortations from the pulpit added new fervour to the fires kindled in the breast of each patriotic citizen.

"It is good to know our cause is one we can ask the blessing of God upon as we stand in his holy temple!" was the only remark made by Leonard on the way home.

They rode silently along among those still and lonely hills, with hearts too full of emotion to think of the greenness and beauty everywhere around them: yet these sweet influences of nature unconsciously affected them, being

> "Still present to the bodily sense,
> Though vanish'd from the thought,"

and operating with a calm and soothing power on their excited minds.

That Sunday evening was one which thousands will remember as the time when they decided what it was their duty to do in that dreadful crisis. Many who volunteered the ensuing week did it, no doubt, from impulse, many from mere love of excitement and adventure, and many others from mercenary motives; but, after making full allowance for all such, there remained a great majority who were actuated by higher considerations.

Well has a foreign writer termed this movement "the uprising of a great people;" for never was a whole nation more deeply stirred. The great body of the citizens through the whole North were kindled into a fervour of patriotic zeal: they believed their country was in danger, and they rushed to the rescue, because they loved that country better than life,— better than all things else on earth.

This conviction was based on a knowledge of the principles on which our government is founded; and it was because they knew the doctrine of secession was but another name for eventual ruin, that they nerved themselves to resist it at all hazards.

# CHAPTER XIX.

### A TALK WITH SUSAN.

It had been a wonderful Sabbath, as we have said; and the evening which followed was also one which will never be forgotten. Many a father that night pressed his children to his bosom with a strange outgush of tenderness, knowing that before another Sunday came he should be away; and many a wife watched her husband's face with an agonizing scrutiny, striving to read there his decision. Some of these wives besought their husbands not to leave them; while others, like Susan Roberts, refrained from a word or even a look that should act as a hindrance in their husbands' way. Still other wives and mothers there were, whose zeal and love of country so lifted them above all personal considerations that they even rejoiced, with that deep, mysterious joy which only heroic souls can understand, to lay their dearest and best-beloved on the altar of their country,—to pour out their life's blood in its defence, if so God should will. Yes, enshrouded in the frail, trembling form of woman, Heaven and its angels beheld many a martyr-soul in those April days.

Susan Roberts was not one of these. She could not rejoice in sacrifice; but she struggled to be submissive, and to forget self in the higher interests involved.

"I am very weak, I believe," she said to Mabel, when the thought of her husband's going to the war first occurred to her, "and a great deal more of a woman than a patriot. I can't help trembling all over at the very thought of Leonard's going; but I will not prevent his doing what he thinks he ought to. I can be brave enough for that; but I can't urge him to go, as some wives do."

During that eventful Sunday she had prayed incessantly for strength from on high; and at evening she felt that her prayers had been answered; for her spirit was now calm, and her faith in God's love so firm, that she fully believed he would carry her safely through any trial which might be before her. After the children were in bed and the whole house quiet, she sat down by her husband, and they calmly discussed the whole subject together.

"I do think, Leonard, I am perfectly willing you should go if it is your duty," she said : "I only want to feel certain in my own mind what your duty is."

"I don't think there can be a doubt of that," said Leonard. "There isn't one in my own mind. If we don't rally now, the traitors who are trying to destroy our government will gain a foothold, which will cost us dear in the future."

"But when I think of what a terrible thing war is, and of what it will bring upon the nation North and South, and that it is the blood of our fellow-citizens—our own brothers, as it were—which we must shed, my soul revolts against it; and I can't help wondering if it really can be right. Oh, Leonard! God must see that a fearful responsibility rests somewhere,—on whoever has brought this war about."

"Fearful! fearful indeed! and I must believe it rests mainly on those Southern demagogues, who, disappointed in obtaining their ends under our government, and undertaking to build up a great Southern Confederacy, have magnified all the grounds of complaint, and inflamed the minds of the people by false representations, till they have really come to believe that they are wronged by the very government which has fostered and upheld them, and so are trying to destroy it,—the best government the world ever saw."

"But was there no way by which a settlement of the difficulties could be brought about without fighting? I want to know that; because, if there was, I should feel that the war was wrong."

"All pacific measures were prevented by their very first act. They went out from us suddenly, claiming that they had a right to go out; they took fraudulent possession of the public property, and then resisted the authority of the government by force, firing on government vessels and government forts. They thus left us no alternative. We must allow that a State has a right to leave the Union in this manner when she chooses, or deny that right. If we had admitted it, our Union would have been lost, all law and order destroyed, and a principle established fatal to all our rights and, eventually, to the existence of the nation itself. Can you not see how this principle lies at the very foundation of our national life? I can; and, for that reason, I feel that every thing sacred and dear to us as a people is now at stake. I feel as strongly as you do that war is a terrible evil,—especially war with our own kindred; and, were the interests involved less vital, I should indeed hesitate before I took up arms. I couldn't conscientiously fight for an increase of territory, nor even, perhaps, to keep what belongs to us. I couldn't fight merely to maintain what is called the balance of power among nations, as is so often done in Europe. But when I think what a blessing our national government has been to us, what peace and freedom and prosperity it has given to us, and what protection to all our rights as citizens, and then reflect what blessings it will continue to give to coming generations, I cannot see it threatened with destruction without lifting my arm to do all I can for its salvation. I abhor war; my whole soul revolts at its horrors; but, if it is ever right to fight for one's country, it must be right to do it now. Nations have often fought for national honour; we fight for national existence."

He paused for a moment, as if overcome with the thoughts which pressed upon him.

"Yes," he said, "there are times when men are called on to sacrifice every thing for their country. Heroism,—patriotism, —these can't be mere names, Susan: they are something real; something God approves of and demands of us. Such a time has come now. Our fathers laid down their lives to secure a country for us, and we must be willing to lay down our's to preserve one for our children. And may God be with us, and give us success, even as he did to them!"

Leonard ceased speaking, and sat for some minutes looking out of the open window into the darkness.

"A mistake here, as you say, Susan, would be dreadful. But I have gone over the ground again and again. I have thought over it, prayed over it, and I can come only to this one result:—that war, even with all its horrors, is better than the ruin of my country. Yes, our cause is a just one; for it is the cause of our country, the cause of freedom, the cause of human rights. I can from my heart pray, '*God save the right!*' Let this comfort you when I am gone. I know it will."

"*When I am gone!*" These words fell mournfully on the heart of the faithful wife, and brought before her all the desolation his absence would bring upon them; and, in spite of her good resolutions, she laid her head on his shoulder and wept bitterly. Leonard understood these tears. They were not rebellious tears, or dissuasives from duty, and he did not attempt to check them, but only folded her closer to his heart. They were a great relief; and when she looked up at him again, it was with her own brave smile.

"I am but a poor wife, I know, for such times as these," she said; "but God will help me to do his will, and I will not be afraid."

## CHAPTER XX.

### VOLUNTEERING.

On Monday afternoon a meeting of the citizens of Woodlee was held. The greatest enthusiasm prevailed, and but one spirit seemed to animate the whole assembly. Even those accustomed to take different sides in politics united now, and vied with each other in their zeal to uphold the Union. Their government and country were alike dear to all, and minor differences were forgotten, now that such vital interests were imperilled. Judge Bailey made one of his most effective speeches, and was followed by his old political opponent, Colonel Towne; and many of the younger men present expressed their views. Among these was Leonard Roberts. He did not talk so fluently as some, but his words carried weight, because they so evidently expressed his real convictions; and when he repeated the charge given him by his grandfather to stand by the old flag, many hearts were touched, for most of them remembered the old gentleman with deep respect, and his words seemed so timely now, they were received with loud cheers. Perhaps no speech of the day exercised a greater influence on the audience than Leonard's; for they all knew his staunch integrity. After pledging themselves to be loyal to the Union, and to do all in their power to sustain it, the meeting adjourned till evening, when all disposed to enlist would have the opportunity, as a military company was to be organized.

On Leonard's return home, he related to the family what had been done.

"Shall you volunteer to-night, Leonard?" asked Susan, quietly.

He met her eye with its clear gaze fixed on his, and for a moment his voice failed him. But he mastered the emotion, and answered, calmly,—

"Yes: I intend to."

Susan's cheek lost its colour for a moment, but she looked up with her own bright smile.

"I could not respect a husband who was not willing to do his duty in such a time as this," she said.

"God bless you, my own brave wife!" cried Leonard. "Now I am strong enough for any thing. I have written to Uncle Roger to ask him to stay here while I am gone. He can look after the farm, and, I think, he will be willing to come. Then Sydney is so near, you know, he can come to mother at any time if she should need him."

While they were at tea, the mail-matter arrived from the office.

"A letter from Sydney to mother," said Leonard. "Tom, you had better take it over to her now;" and he eagerly glanced over the daily paper.

"I think Washington is safe now, Susan: so many troops have arrived there, they will not dare to attack it."

"That is a great relief," said Susan.

"Yes, indeed; and the whole country is roused. Just hear what the merchants in our cities are doing!" And he read aloud how they were everywhere coming forward with munificent offers to the government of pecuniary assistance.

"Oh, father! grandmother wants you to come over there this minute," cried Tom, rushing in breathless. "Uncle Sydney has gone to be a soldier!"

Leonard went to her immediately. She was too much agitated to speak, but handed him the letter, which was as follows:—

"Dear Mother:—You will be surprised —not sorry, I hope—to hear I have enlisted, and am to leave for New York to-night. A company was formed here, and quite a number of our class have joined it. There was no time to gain your consent; but I am sure, mother, you would have given it. I know you would not have your boys disgrace their father's memory; and Leonard ought not to go, for you all need him at home. But I can be spared as well as not. Indeed, I *must* go; for to stay here with this fire burning in my heart, would be impossible.

"Do not feel anxious about me. God's blessing will go with me; for I go to fight in a righteous cause. I am willing to die for my country, if it is so ordered: yet I hope I may come back and get a *welcome home* from you and Mabel. But God's will be done!

"Love to Leonard and Susan, and a kiss for the babies. I hope they will never have cause to blush for their uncle or their country. God bless you all! I go at six to-night. Every thing is furnished us, the ladies having sewed night and day to get our clothing ready. Good-by. I will write again soon.

"Sydney."

This was indeed startling intelligence. They had prepared their minds to give Leonard up, but had never once thought that Sydney could go.

"He isn't fit to go," said his mother,— "no more fit than a baby. He never can stand the fatigue of marching. If he were only well and strong, I wouldn't say one word; but——"

"He is in God's holy keeping," said Leonard, hopefully, "and there we must leave him. God bless the dear fellow!" he added; "it was just like him to follow a noble impulse without hesitating. God bless him, I say again!"

"But a fit of enthusiasm won't carry him through the hardships of a campaign," said his mother. "He will give out on the road, and die without accomplishing any thing."

So predicted many a mother whose youngest boy had left college for the field, fired by an irresistible ardour; and many a sister answered as Mabel did:—

"A strong soul sometimes does wonders even for the body, mother; and you know Sydney is much better than he used to be."

"This is, indeed, a costly sacrifice, dear mother," said Leonard. "Your youngest and your best,—your gifted one. But it is made in a righteous cause, and God will accept it according to its value. He knows how much it costs you. These are the days when nothing can be withheld from our country, and nothing is too precious to give for its salvation."

"If he had come home, you would not have refused your consent?" said Mabel.

"No, I should not have dared to take that responsibility; but I should have advised him not to go. It is only because I am afraid he is not strong enough," she said; "but it is God's will, and I will not murmur. I have asked Him to make me willing to sacrifice all he required of me; and my children were given to God long years ago. They are his now, not mine."

"Yes, his to be used for a high and holy purpose, mother, such as he will bless."

Leonard knelt with them in prayer, commending the beloved son and brother and their dear country to God's watchful, tender keeping, and beseeching for each trembling, anguished heart through all the land strength, guidance and comfort from on high.

The mother's heart was somewhat calmed; but she could not sleep. It was a night of wrestling prayer,—such a night as had never before been known in the red house, amidst all the trials and changes that had taken place under its roof; but *the Comforter* still abode there, and sustained the souls that called on him.

When Leonard returned from the meeting, he told his wife he had not enlisted. "I am not sure I ought to go, now Sydney has left us," he said; "for I depended on him to look after mother. I ought not to act rashly; and I shall wait a little before finally deciding."

"Are many going from here?"

"Yes. It is wonderful to see the spirit our young men show. I feel proud of them! I think there will be no want of men: if there should be, I should go, of course. It ought to have been me, and not Sydney; for, as mother says, he hasn't the strength to make a good soldier."

"His going is a terrible blow to mother," said Susan. "She tries to bear it bravely; but I have never seen her so overcome by any thing."

"Yes, he has always been her favourite; indeed, the favourite of us all. I regret his going myself, because physical strength is worth more to a private soldier than the finest mind; but it can't be helped now, and we must decide what we ought to do. It does seem to me that if there are as many volunteers as the government wants, I had better stay at home through this summer at least. By fall I could get my business arranged so that I could leave it much more easily. But the country comes first; and, if we find more men are needed, I must leave you and mother alone, trusting that you will be taken care of."

The weeks that followed, who does not remember them?—the weeks when banners floated on every breeze, when the sound of the drum was heard in every village, and companies of young men were everywhere seen drilling at home or hurrying off to camps for more thorough training. In an hour, as it were, the nation which had been lapped in the profoundest peace became a nation of soldiers, and the enthusiasm which prevailed lifted men above not only the fear of death, but almost above all thought of suffering or disaster. It was a wonderful spectacle, and one most beautiful in its aspect of self-sacrifice and love of country. But there was an undue self-exaltation, an overweening spirit of confidence in our ability to do whatever we undertook, that could not be justified when we were only girding on our armour for the conflict. Who dreamed then of disaster and defeat? How proudly and bravely our young sons and brothers talked with flashing eyes of success and victory! And fond mothers and sisters cheered them on, almost as hopeful as they,—the bright, enthusiastic youths whose bones were to whiten every battle-field from the Potomac to the Mississippi! But they were a gallant band, those first young volunteers; and, though they had the false confidence of youth and inexperience, their spirit of lofty enthusiasm was good to see, and the nation mourns for them as for her beautiful, her well-beloved, and holds their memory as something to be cherished and kept sacred through all coming time. When we remember them as they went forth in those summer-days, so fresh, so fair, so hopeful, and then think of all they endured in the battle-field and hospital, our hearts recoil with an agony too fearful, too real, to be expressed in words.

But they went forth from pure and

exalted motives. They were given up by their friends in a spirit no less pure and noble. They were followed by untold prayers and blessings; and we know their blood has not been shed in vain. It was not for nought that weeping and desolation came into all our dwellings, and the cry of anguish went up from thousands of childless mothers into the ear of the God of hosts. No sacrifice which is made for a righteous principle is ever made in vain. The soul is always ennobled by it and brought nearer to Him who gave himself a sacrifice for many; and we know the desolate hearts that weep for their lost ones have become tenderer, nobler and stronger than they could have been without this baptism of blood and agony. God grant that we, who are now a nation of mourners, may become also a nation of penitents, purified through suffering,—a nation fearing God and keeping his commandments!

Letters frequently came to the red house

from Sydney, written in such fine spirits as to cheer all their hearts. At first he was stationed at Arlington Heights, but afterwards removed to Fortress Monroe, and was among the troops that took a part in the fight at Big Bethel. He never complained of the hardships of his new life, but, on the contrary, said he was never so vigorous, and that he believed the hard fare and out-of-door life were just what he needed to make a man of him.

"Since I came here," he wrote to Leonard, "I have found out what I was designed for; and what do you think it is? Why, for a surgeon. I know you will laugh, and that you and Mabel will put your wise heads together and talk about my weak nerves and my inability to bear excitement, and all that; but I am in earnest, and if I ever go home I shall certainly study medicine and surgery. After the fight at Big Bethel, I assisted, as I wrote you, in bringing in the wounded;

"The surgeon said I was a right handy fellow, who took hold in the right spot."  p. 283.

and, as there were very few assistant surgeons, I was detailed to do duty in the hospital. I witnessed dreadful scenes there, I assure you,—crushed and mangled bodies, broken limbs, and horrid gun-shot wounds of every description. To my amazement, I found myself perfectly calm and my nerves as steady as a clock; and I also found that I had an aptitude for doing what was required of me, or, as the surgeon said, was 'a right handy fellow, who took hold in the right spot.' You used to laugh at me on the farm for being so awkward in using the tools, and so I was. I always took up a hoe or rake wrong end first; but I handle broken limbs and bandages famously, I can assure you.

"I have been in the hospital, more or less, ever since, and it has been a real delight to me, if I may use the word in such a connection; but I do enjoy it, because I know I am alleviating suffering. The poor fellows are so grateful for even a kind word, that I often think I should be willing to be a hospital-nurse all my life; but, as I hope the war won't last many years, I should soon get out of employment. There are a great many opportunities for doing good here,—I mean to souls as well as bodies. The old barriers which keep men apart in society are broken down, and we come together face to face, soul to soul. You know I never could pray in a public-meeting; but I lose all my nervous timidity when I kneel down by some dying soldier: I forget every thing then but God's presence and the wants of that poor fellow-creature. Yes, God does seem very near us in the midst of these terrible scenes, and one feels like praying as he never did before. They say familiarity with death lessens its solemnity; but I doubt if any man could be in one of these hospitals and not feel the need of something beyond human help.

\* \* \* \* \* \*

"Yes, my heart has been enlarged and my tongue loosed; and I want you to tell mother that I never before felt so sure I was in my right placé as I do now. So she must thank God I came, instead of worrying about me. I am as well as I can be. To be sure, I may get sick, or I may be killed; but I shall have the satisfaction of knowing I tried to do my duty, which, I take it, is worth more to a man, living or dying, than any thing else. I should write you oftener, but I am very busy. I have written a good many letters for the sick: sad and touching enough some of them were. Many a poor fellow's heart is yearning for home and home-friends as he lies on his little cot; but generally the sick are wonderfully patient. More than once I have taken last messages from some poor boy, and then written his mother of his death. This is sad work; and yet the blessing of some of these poor fellows lies warm at my heart. I have not a wish to be anywhere but where I am: let that comfort you, dear friends, if any thing should happen to me."

\* \* \* \* \* \*

Leonard continued to work on the farm quietly through the summer-months; for, as there were plenty of volunteers to meet the requisition of the President, he believed it was his duty to stay at home. Occasionally some townsman would ill-naturedly remark,

"There's Leonard Roberts; all his fine talk about patriotism don't amount to much. Why don't he enlist, if he cares so much for the country?"

But, so long as he knew he did care for his country, he was not annoyed. To have his heart right before God was his main desire; and he believed he was loyal in His sight. So he kept on working and hoping. But when the news came of the Bull-Run defeat, even Leonard's strong faith was sorely shaken for a time: it was so unexpected, so humiliating, so terrible!

"If our troops hadn't run, I could have

borne it," said Mabel, as they sat gloomily talking over the details. "Defeat would have been nothing, but *disgrace!* oh, Leonard," she cried, covering her face with her hands, "I don't feel as if I could ever look on the old flag again. It has been disgraced. The stars and stripes lie trailing in the dust! I believe it will break my heart."

"Other troops and better-disciplined ones than our's have fled in a panic," he answered; "but it is dreadful. The worst of it is, it makes us doubt whether our volunteers will make good soldiers; and we have no others; we must rely on them. I believe, though, they will yet prove themselves worthy of confidence. I can't believe Yankee boys can ever be cowards!"

"Do you suppose God can be on their side?" asked Mabel, despondingly. "Is he going to suffer the nation to be destroyed?"

"On their side? No, Mabel, *no! He* on the side of treachery and slavery?—

*never!* Whatever else is false, God is true. He may suffer wickedness to prosper for a time, as he often has in the world's history; but approve of their course,—that he never can! No, let defeat and ruin come, I will still keep my faith in Him,—still feel that there is one rock unmoved amid all the billows that are overwhelming us!"

"We have been an arrogant and sinful nation," said Mrs. Roberts. "We need chastisement, and I hope we shall receive it in a right spirit. Let us humble ourselves under the mighty hand of God, and turn away from our iniquities, and see if the Lord will not bless and save us."

"Yes, we are a sinful nation," said Leonard. "Though I believe we are right in this contest, we are wicked and deserve rebuke: there is no doubt of that. If we are not guilty of the same sins as the men of the South, we have committed others just as heinous, it may be, in the sight of a just God, as their's."

That was a dark day,—a day in which the light in many souls went out and they sat in darkness and the shadow of death. But in time the cloud disappeared, and men once more looked up and walked erect. All was not lost, and every loyal citizen felt that, instead of yielding to despair, he must rouse himself to new efforts; and so the call for more men was met as promptly, if not as exultingly, as before. New regiments flocked to the camps, and wives, mothers and sisters again consecrated their bravest and best-beloved to the cause, with an enthusiasm less noisy, perhaps, but still more deep and earnest than at first. The fearful nature of war was better understood, but the confidence they felt in the justice of their cause was stronger than ever; and this raised them above all cowardly misgivings. It was very touching to see fathers and mothers whose sons were lying buried under Southern soil or in prison at Richmond, now sending off others with prayers and blessings as bravely as at first.

Again Leonard considered the question of enlisting. Had there been any want of men, he would not have hesitated a single moment; but as many were enlisting as the government had called for or could arm : so he decided to stay at home and gather in his crops. But he put every thing in readiness to leave, if it should become necessary; and he neglected nothing that could be done for the country at home. He contributed liberally to the fund raised for the families of the volunteers ; and each member of his family was an active worker for the hospitals. Not one was idle : each could do something,—grandmother, mother and children, old and young, could sew or knit, or scrape lint, or pick berries, for the soldiers; and each was willing to go without every thing not absolutely essential, that they might send something to the sick and wounded who were away from home and all home-comforts.

Thus the months wore away and the year 1861 closed; alas! how mournfully in many a bereaved household,—how anxiously in all! for few could forget, even if their own loved ones were safe, how many others had fallen, and still must fall before the war was ended!

## CHAPTER XXI.

### THE NEW CAPTAIN.

IN the summer of the succeeding year, 1862, a call was made for additional volunteers. This was not responded to so enthusiastically as the previous ones, partly because a feeling of despondency was creeping over the land, and partly because those most likely to enlist had already done so. This was the time for truly loyal souls to trim their lamps and keep their faith in God and their cause burning. The timid and the wavering, of course, lost hope; and some who if success had crowned our cause would have been considered loyal citizens, turned false to it, and joined hands with traitors. In all great undertakings there comes such a turning-point; and then the metal of which souls are made is tested.

Leonard's was one to ring back true and clear. If the feeble-minded were predicting ruin, and the false-hearted proving treacherous, he considered it so much the more necessary that all true lovers of their country should come to the rescue. If the enemy were crossing the Potomac and likely to take Washington, so much the more reason why the army should be strengthened, instead of men's staying at home and grumbling at the government and the generals, even if they had made great mistakes, as very likely, being fallible men, they had. The goodness of the cause did not, with him, depend on the measure of its success. If it was right to defend the Union from dissolution at first, it was right to defend it now; and defend it he would, so far as lay in his power.

"This is the first time since the commencement of the war that there has been any lack of volunteers," he said to Susan. "I have always said I should go when there was; and I have decided to go now. There is a meeting to-night for forming another company in the —— regiment. I shall join that, I think."

The words were spoken in a more business-like tone than they would have been a year before, and his wife heard them more calmly; but whether it was in reality any easier to bear the trial of parting it would be dificult to say. She was more willing he should go, because she saw more clearly the necessity for it, and because a year of sacrifices had enlarged her heart and made the cause for which she had prayed and laboured still more sacred and dear; but she also knew better the dangers to which he was exposing himself; for by that time the first vague idea of war and its evils had given way to a sadly accurate comprehension of its horrors.

After Leonard went to the meeting, she sat alone, sewing steadily as ever; but her fancy was busy drawing painful pictures of what her husband might suffer in camps or hospitals, for she had come to dread the latter almost more than the actual battle-field, so many had died in them. But, in spite of this, her heart rested calmly on God and his overruling providence. She believed that he had laid on this generation the settlement of great questions, and that it was far nobler to suffer for the right and to lay down life for it, even, than to live in ease at home.

"Your faith would fail, if it was *your* husband who was going," was what the wife of a soldier, whom she was trying to comfort, had once said to her. "I tell you, faith gives out when the time comes."

But Susan's faith did not give out. Genuine faith never does, but burns brighter and fills the soul with warmth and courage just when they are most needed. When Leonard came home, they discussed their plans very quietly. Uncle Roger was to come and have the direction of the business. He would not be able to do much work, but he was an excellent manager, and the hired man was trusty and faithful. The volunteers were to go into camp in a few days; but, as it was only six miles from Woodlee, Leonard hoped to be able to come home once or twice before their final departure. His enlistment was for three years or during the war; the regiment to which his company belonged being one of the last which was filled up before the call for nine-months men was made.

To Leonard's surprise, the company proposed to make him their captain; but he at once declined, giving as a reason his total ignorance of all military matters: indeed, he had never drilled before in his life, except under the direction of an old militia-captain. But Colonel Towne and several other influential citizens urged him to accept, assuring him he was better fitted for the command than any other man in the company. So far as courage and intelligence were concerned, he doubtless was;

and, as the colonel laughingly said, "They were all pretty much on the same level, if familiarity with military tactics was to be taken into the account." Finding that the knowledge requisite could be acquired in the camp, where they were expected to remain some time, and perhaps aware himself that no man would be more conscientious in discharging the duties of the position, he at last consented to take the command. The company was composed of one hundred and one men, forty of whom belonged to Woodlee, and all of them were well known to Leonard.

Serious as the feelings of all parties were at this juncture, Susan could not forbear an occasional joke about her husband's military honours; indeed, she seemed determined that his last few days at home should be as cheerful as possible. Once having settled that a certain course of action was right, Leonard himself was always calm in pursuing it; and no one who had seen him in his own home or in the red house would have dreamed he was preparing for any thing more than an ordinary journey. The old flag waved gayly from its accustomed point, and he never caught a glimpse of it without feeling a warmer glow at his heart. "I am true to it," he would say to himself. "I am willing to lay down my life for it, as grandfather charged me." But he seldom said even this aloud.

Nothing that could be done by him to make the two families comfortable during his absence was forgotten; no little arrangement overlooked. He also quietly talked with Susan of what he wanted done in his business, and in regard to the children, if he never came back,—for neither of them shrank from looking the future fairly in the face; and even the mother, now she was to part from her last son, seemed far more cheerful and calm than when Sydney left her. It is a noticeable fact, that during the war those who have made the fewest sacrifices for their country are those who complain most of the hardships of the war;

while those who have given their children, and even buried the most precious of them in its service, are those who are looking forward with the greatest composure and hopefulness to the final result. That for which we have made sacrifices we love: those who have given most to their country love it best.

It was a pleasant day in August when Leonard and his company marched to the music of a brass-band from Woodlee to the camp. Forming on the green at Woodlee centre, they passed directly by the red house, and the children of both families were thrown into the most joyful excitement by the music, and the sight of "the pretty soldiers," as Charlie called them. Leonard dared not trust himself to look towards the house. One glance at the old flag, and up at the clear heavens above it, was all he gave in that direction; but above the tread of feet and the noise of drums and fifes he heard a gleeful, childish shout, "There's my pa-pa!" Blinding tears rushed to his eyes; for Leonard was a tender father, and Charlie was his pet and pride; but he dashed them away, and only vowed the more earnestly to do all he could to preserve a free and undivided country for his boys to dwell in.

The —— regiment was summoned to the seat of war much sooner than was expected, and Leonard only came home once after going into camp. Fortunately, the precise time for their leaving was not then known; for, though Leonard was pretty certain in his own mind he should not come home again, the doubt prevented a last farewell. The last day of his stay, he was detained in the centre of the town by business till after dark; and, as he came past the burying-ground on his way home, an irresistible impulse led him to open the little white gate and seek his grandfather's grave. A plain marble slab marked it, bearing, besides his name and age, only this simple inscription:—

"LOYAL TO GOD AND HIS COUNTRY."

Leonard stood some minutes beside it, lost in thought. He went back to the days of his childhood, and remembered the talks of the old gentleman, and his earnest desire to have his descendants loyal to the country he had loved so well himself. Then he thought of the changes that had come over this country, and how the whole land was now filled with violence and blood,—torn asunder and rent by faction and hatred and wild, fierce passions. It was a dreadful picture to contemplate in that stillness; and now he himself was about to mingle in the fray and to shed his brothers' blood,—very likely to lose his own life in the contest! It was a trying moment; and had Leonard's convictions of duty been based on any thing less firm, or been more hastily formed, they might have given way. But he had carefully made up his mind; and, terrible as the alternative was, he was confident that no choice was left to a man who loved his country and the principles on which its government was founded, but to fight now for their maintenance. "Yes," he said, looking up fearlessly into the heavens, with nothing between his soul and God's eye of truth, "there can be no mistake. I am fighting for a cause which God approves,—the cause of justice, of freedom, of human rights. His blessing will go with me, and I will not fear what men can do unto me."

Then, reverently uncovering his head and kneeling on the grave, he prayed that he too might live and die loyal to God and to his country, and loyal to the great principles of eternal justice which underlie God's throne and uphold all righteous human governments. When he rose and looked up to the sky, now gleaming with myriads of bright stars, he almost believed he could see his grandfather's face smiling approvingly upon him, and hear him again saying, "You can be a patriot, Leonard God grant you always may be!" "I should hardly dare to meet you in another world, dear grandfather," he murmured, "if I had failed to do my duty in this crisis. I know if you were living, you would have sent me to fight under the old flag, perhaps long ago."

As he walked home beneath the starlight, he looked earnestly at each familiar object—the hills, the trees, and rocks—with a consciousness that probably it was his last look; and it was wonderful even to himself how calmly he could do it, and of how little consequence life seemed when weighed against such tremendous interests as were now involved.

His mind ran backward over his past life. Thirty-two years he had lived: years of labour and hardship, but also years of great tranquillity and enjoyment, had they been. God's blessing had rested on the labour of his hands, and he believed it would rest on him still. Oh, how earnestly in that hour did he bless God for the hope that when he was called away from this life, it would not be to death and annihilation, but to a higher life and to nobler service: so that if the call came soon and suddenly, he need fear no evil, because the same God who had hitherto blessed him would still be his stay and portion forever. With the sailor-boy who so many years ago had passed from the bosom of the ocean to the bosom of God, he could say, "I know God can take care of me just as well in another world as in this." How, then, could he fear to die in a righteous cause?

He saw how this faith in God had been the blessing of his whole life,—how through that all knowledge had been hallowed, all toil ennobled, and all home-joys made sweet and sacred. Heartily, too, he thanked God for giving him pious and loyal ancestors, who had taught him to love God and his country; and his soul glowed with a consciousness that he was not wholly unworthy to be their descendant, but was now permitted to show that he too loved the country they had left him for an inheritance. That hour, so calm, so full of deep emotion, in spite of the uncertainty and the impending separation, was not a gloomy one to Leonard, but rather one of heartfelt thanksgiving,—an hour made sacred by that solemn joy vouchsafed by God only to those who leave all to follow him.

It was comparatively easy for the man and the patriot to give his life for his country; but for the father, the sacrifice was much more difficult. As he came in sight of the two cottages nestled so peacefully under the green trees, and thought of their inmates,—the mother who bore him, the wife of his bosom, the children of his love,—and of how desolate and unprotected they would be if he should die, a sharp pang shot through his heart. But even above this fear, faith could carry him triumphantly. Desolate, with God for their father and friend! Unprotected, with the arm of the Almighty for their shield and buckler! He took shame to himself for the thought; and, while his heart thrilled to its very core with inexpressible tenderness for them, he laid them, too, in the arms of the loving Father without one fear,—the Father who was so much wiser and more loving than he, and who would "never leave them nor forsake them."

At home, the same animating faith was lifting up the souls of his wife and mother; and while they were thus able to give themselves and each other into God's keeping, they could be calm and hopeful. "*Thou wilt keep him in perfect peace whose mind is stayed on thee, because he trusteth in thee.*" This promise so graciously made, the faithful soul always finds is kept: the only difficulty is that in hours of trial and temptation our souls are too rarely "stayed on God," and hence fail to enjoy the "perfect peace" promised by Him who cannot lie.

## CHAPTER XXII.

### ARMY LETTERS.

THE regiment to which Leonard belonged was ordered to join the Army of the Potomac. They reached their destination in safety, after the usual amount of discomfort by the way; and every week brought a letter from the captain, either to his wife or mother. It was a time of despondency in many hearts, those early autumn months of 1862; but he always wrote in good spirits, and with a hearty confidence in God and the cause he was fighting for. Yet, in spite of this, Susan's faith sometimes faltered; and in one of her letters to her husband she wrote, " I could bear all this terrible sacrifice of life if there were only a prospect that the country would be saved by it; but I can't bear to think that all this precious blood is being shed in vain."

In reply, Leonard wrote, "I know perfectly well, my dear wife, that you have faith enough in God to trust yourself and your children and me in his hands, to be disposed of as he shall see best, and you feel certain he will do what is right by us all. Now, can't you leave your country also in his hands, and feel just as sure that he will do what is right by *that?* I think I can; though for a good while after the commencement of the war, when I thought of the bare possibility of our failure, I rebelled against it, and said, 'I can submit to any thing else, but not to see my country disgraced and ruined.' But should we not be as willing God should reign among the nations, as in our families? He does reign, and will accomplish his purposes, whether we are willing or not; and if we are true Christians we shall feel so certain that these purposes are just and righteous ones, that we shall rejoice in their fulfilment even where they cross our wishes. We are such very short-sighted creatures that we may desire for our country what God sees would be an injury to it, or an injury to the best interests of humanity. So let us rejoice that it is his will, and not our's, which is to be done. The cause of freedom, of civilization, of human happiness, is not going backwards in this nineteenth century. God will take care of that, and in his own way insure its success. Let what will be the result of this war, the great principles of freedom and righteousness for which we contend are safe—safe now and forever—in God's keeping. This certainty keeps one from discouragement under all reverses,—some of which are hard enough to bear, I admit. I believe our cause will finally succeed, because I think our triumph will be the triumph of right principles. But we are a very sinful nation; and when I see how much fraud and corruption there is everywhere among us, I sometimes think we deserve to perish:

at any rate, we deserve severe chastisement, and shall doubtless receive it. And, if by that means we may be made better and more honest, let us welcome the discipline as the fire which is to refine and purify us and make us a nation fit to serve God and benefit the world. If we do all we can to preserve our country firm on its old basis of union and constitutional liberty, and then fail, we shall not be to blame. I don't believe we *shall* fail; but I wish to stay your soul and mine on something firmer than any human government,—even on the eternal love and justice of the great Jehovah."

At another time he wrote as follows:—

"You know, dear mother, how I liked to watch the stars when I was a child; and now when I am on duty I enjoy it more than ever. What a host of memories sometimes come over me as I look at them; they are so associated with you all, and with the dear old hills around Woodlee. I know they are shining on the old homestead, and I can see just how quietly the red house and the white cottage are standing there in the deep shadows. I am never homesick; I have never for a moment regretted coming; but I sometimes feel a great longing to see you all. Still, if a wish would take me back, I would not go. No, I am glad to be doing my part in this conflict,—glad to give one life, if it is needed, for the good cause. The Woodlee boys are a fine set of fellows, and I feel proud of them. I laughed heartily over that letter of Russell's to the London Times, in which he seems so shocked to find that the privates in our army are on hand-shaking terms with their captain, and saying, 'How dy'e do?' to him, just as if he were one of themselves. Just imagine me giving myself airs, and refusing to be familiar with my old neighbours and friends! I mean they shall obey my orders promptly and to the letter; and they do it all the more readily that they know me well and have always been on familiar, hand-shaking terms with me. My men are too intelligent to take advantage of this intimacy; but some regiments are made up of men who need keeping down. They haven't self-respect enough to know their place except when they are made to. But our New England boys, those from country towns especially, are of a different stamp. As I say, I am proud of my company, for they are almost without exception steady, intelligent, moral young men, and many of them religious men, who are glad to have a service on Sunday and a prayer-meeting in the week; both which I always attend if possible.

"But star-gazing brings other thoughts, too,—thoughts of how infinite God is, and of how his mind grasps all worlds and all periods of time. Why, we think because one little part of our planet is in a tumult now, that all is confusion. But there are these millions of worlds moving on in their orbits just as calmly and peacefully as ever, and God is quietly watching over them and over us all.

> "'Thy throne eternal ages stood
> Ere seas or stars were made :
> Thou art the ever-living God,
> Were all the nations dead.'

"That is a grand old hymn of Watts's. Do sing it once in a while, or, rather, sing it every Sunday night. I shall like to think of you as all joining in it to old Mear. I always fancy you are singing Sunday nights, just as we used to. I hope you miss my tenor a little; but Uncle Roger can give you a glorious bass, which will more than make it up. To sing these old hymns from the heart will do you all good.

"You will smile when I tell you I am studying astronomy. There is a good deal of time when we are not on drill; and my old habit of taking up a book at odd moments clings to me yet. Among the books sent to the hospital—a curious collection of old rubbish from somebody's garret—I found an old school-book on astronomy, well thumbed and soiled; and, as nobody wanted it, I brought it to my tent, and am making my way through it by degrees, taking observations of the sky at night, and sometimes getting a look through the telescope at the observatory, the officers there being very kind and civil to me. We try all ways to beguile the time in camp; and this is much more to my taste than the card-playing so many indulge in."

Not only from Leonard himself, but from the letters of his men to their families, his wife got news of him very frequently: these latter told how firm he was in enforcing discipline, how thoughtful of their comfort, and how much they all respected and loved him.

"Ah, yes," said his old teacher, Miss Brace, when she had listened to one of these letters, "Leonard Roberts knew how to obey,—the first requisite for a good commander: he was such a truthful, honest boy, I always knew he would make a first-rate man."

They heard often from Sydney, too. He had been slightly wounded in two battles,—for he had been in all the battles before Richmond, and in the retreat which followed,—but had recovered, and he wrote in the autumn that his health was never better. One of his old college-tutors received a letter from his colonel, speaking in the highest terms of his labours among the sick and wounded, and of his holding meetings for the well, as well as reading and praying with the sick and dying.

"He is worth more than half our chaplains, so far as the souls of the men are concerned," wrote the colonel; "for he is always doing good somewhere, when off duty. You wouldn't know him now for the puny, bashful senior who enlisted eighteen months ago. He looks bluff and hearty as any man among us."

Yes, strange as it would have seemed if any one had predicted it, the pale, delicate, sensitive lad had found his right place in the army; and his powers, physical and mental, had developed into a manlier and healthier growth than they would have reached anywhere else. The excellent home-training received in the old red house showed its fruits now; and the mother who had simply aimed at making them industrious, honest, God-fearing boys, rejoiced to find they had both become courageous and useful men, who were doing good service to their country.

So the months wore away; and the inmates of the red house were quiet and usually hopeful. The gray locks on Mary Roberts's brow grew grayer still, but her blue eye retained its old brightness; and she gathered her five grandchildren around her in the little parlour, and showed them the ostrich-eggs and corals and the beautiful sea-shells, and told them stories about the wonderful islands that lie bathed in sunshine far out on the bosom of the great ocean, just as she had told them to their parents; and they listened just as eagerly, and asked for more stories just as perseveringly. Sometimes they tired her; but still their childish mirth and prattle kept her heart young and fresh.

The little orphans, Mary and Mabel (for so their mother had named them, though they called the little one May, to distinguish her from Aunt Mabel), grew up into two sweet little girls, so much alike in size that strangers often thought they were twins; and never had the roof of the red house rang to merrier songs and shouts than now, when Tom and Charlie joined their plays; and at night, when tired of play, and gentle and loving as two little doves, the little girls knelt down by their trundle-bed to say their "good-night prayers to God," as May called it, the hearts of both aunt and grandmother rejoiced over them greatly.

"What a blessing these children have been to us!" they often said to each other. "How could we have lived without them?"

Uncle Roger gathered in the crops, and looked after the out-door work; and within and without things went on more smoothly and more after the old way than they could have believed possible. Of course, there was a great anxiety always lying at the bottom of their hearts, but their faith in God kept it from degenerating into a worrying, fretful state of mind; and so they might be said to be quite cheerful, patiently waiting for whatever the future was destined to bring.

Just before the battle of Fredericksburg, they received a letter from Leonard, from which we make the following extract:—

"Who do you think was brought in by one of our pickets last night? A deserter from the rebels,—and a more haggard, dirty-looking fellow we do not often see. He was brought to my tent; but, as I was busy looking over some accounts, I took no notice at first, till, hearing some one say, 'He's 'most gone: he's well-nigh starved to death,' I ordered some food given to him, and, seeing how miserably ill he looked, I had some tea taken from my own stores, some of that you sent me,—a thousand thanks for it,—and told them to make him a good strong cup, and returned to my writing again. This revived the poor fellow wonderfully. It was the first tea and sugar he had seen for six months, as I afterwards heard him say. He was soon able to eat some toast that Jim Baker had fixed up for him. Jim makes a famous cook, I assure you, and contrives all kinds of savoury messes out of nothing. Something in the man's voice, as he spoke, struck me, and I looked at him closer, but could discover nothing familiar in the grimy face covered by a monstrous beard. 'Why, you don't know me!' he exclaimed; 'but I knew you as quick as I set my eyes on you, Lenny Roberts,—or Captain Roberts, as I see they call you now. How are they all at the old red house? And the Woodlee boys,—I see lots of 'em are here. Can't make me out? It's because I've got these clothes on!'

"'It can't be John Hall!' I exclaimed. 'Yes, John Hall, at your service, captain,' he answered, with a loud laugh. I knew he went South soon after leaving Woodlee, and commenced practising law in Mobile; but I had heard nothing of him for several years. 'Yes, I fight under the stars and bars,' he cried, in a kind of mocking, excited way; 'and you stick to the old flag yet. Ha! I guess you remember how the old captain used to get it out Fourth of Julys and tell the boys to be loyal to it, and all that stuff?'

"I didn't much fancy such a disrespectful style of talk, and said, half angrily, 'Well, John, it would have been better for you if you had followed his advice, I'm thinking.' 'May-be 'twould,' he said, in the same reckless way; 'but, you see, a body has to do as other folks do. When I first went South I stood up for the Yankees whenever anybody run 'em down; but, you see, a fellow couldn't get along there in that way. Mobile is a famous place for a fellow to get on, if he keeps his

"'It can't be John Hall!' I exclaimed." p. 320.

mouth shut. I got into a capital practice there, and by-and-by I married a rich girl. So, you see, I was getting on swimmingly, till this infernal war broke out. I had to go with the South, of course, if I stayed there, and I couldn't get away with my property lying in "live stock," you know. I held off from fighting, though, as long as I could; but I had to enlist to save myself from something worse. I've fought in half a dozen battles, but was never hurt till I got shot in the leg the other day. I was left behind, and have been lying round here these ten days, so lame I could scarcely crawl, and half starved besides: so I crept up towards the pickets to-night, hoping to find something here to eat, and who should I come on pat but a Connecticut regiment! and, thinks I, "I'll show myself, and see what they'll say to an old friend. I can't do any worse than lie here and starve, any way." So the fellow I hailed brought me in here, right among old friends, as 'twere.'

"In a little while he begged for whiskey; but, as none of our boys keep that, he was obliged to content himself with tea. He finally fell into a doze, and slept all night. This morning he was quite ill, and seemed in a high fever; and I have sent him to the hospital, and shall see that he is well cared for. I must give him up to my superior officer when he gets well, if he ever does. Poor John! he was always ambitious and had talent, but I fear he was never willing to work and *earn* reputation and success; and he was too anxious to be popular, to stand up very staunchly for the right. I fear he has become dissipated; but it may be only the effects of illness and exposure. His style of talk was exceedingly repulsive; but I feel kindly towards him for old acquaintance' sake. How little we thought of meeting thus, when we went to school together and laid our plans for future life! It would have broken his parents' hearts to know he was in the rebel army; but they are both gone now. I sometimes think people are spared a great deal by dying, now-a-days."

The same mail brought a letter from Sydney, telling them that his regiment had been ordered to join a division in General Burnside's army, and that a decisive battle was no doubt to be fought soon. "We are ready for it," he said, "and I think our boys will all do their best. Of course, it must bring death to thousands of us; and I need not say, dear mother, my heart turns more warmly to you to-night for this certainty. If I fall, I shall fall doing my duty, and I believe Christ will take me to himself; not for any thing good in me, but because I have put my trust in him, and he will never break his promise to save all who have done that. I never felt more convinced that I did right in coming; and I hope I shall do my duty bravely to the last. We shall soon meet, here, or on the other side, as God wills. God bless you all!"

## CHAPTER XXIII.

### BATTLE OF FREDERICKSBURG.

THE battle which followed was one most disastrous to the North, and which brought into thousands of homes bitter sorrow and lamentation. But in no battle of the war did the Northern troops show more heroic bravery. Again and again were they brought up to face the intrenched foe, and were mowed down like grass. Again and again they rallied to the charge, but all in vain; and, amid a carnage unrivalled even in this bloody war, they were compelled to fall back, and retreat across the Rappahannock.

It was a dark, stormy night when the news of the battle reached the red house, but Susan went over, as usual, to read the paper aloud to her mother and Mabel. The first accounts left it uncertain what the result would be, but showed that it had been a fiercely-fought battle, and that the two regiments to which Leonard and Sydney belonged were both engaged. Then came the long, weary waiting, the agony of suspense: how fearful, none can ever know but such as have experienced it. Two days and nights dragged wearily away, every hour seeming like a month. With trembling hands they opened each day's paper, and their hearts stood still as they looked over the long lists of killed and wounded; and they breathed a long sigh of relief when the end was reached and the name not there. Those were hours—that was agony—harder to bear than any thing which had gone before. The first news of the Woodlee boys came through a telegram from Leonard. He was unhurt; but three of his company were killed, others wounded, but not severely. Sydney was among the missing,—whether killed, wounded, or a prisoner, it was impossible to say. A joyful "Thank God!" escaped from Susan's lips when she found Leonard was safe; but she instantly reproached herself when she remembered that Sydney might be slain, and that two other wives in the neighbourhood were widows if she were not.

Three days after, came another telegram:—

"*Sydney went from earth to heaven this morning at nine o'clock. He died in my arms, without a groan.*"

The long suspense was ended now; certainty had taken the place of dread. They knew now that one of their beloved ones could never come to them again. It was a heavy blow, especially to the mother; and it was of her, not of themselves, that both the good daughters first thought. They feared she would sink under it; but, instead of this, she bore it very bravely, and soon became calm and peaceful, and able to look at all that was consoling in the circumstances.

"Dear boy!" she said, tenderly, "I know

he is in heaven; I can't have a doubt of that: he is where no sorrow nor pain can ever reach him more."

"Yes, mother; and, if he could speak to us from there, it would be to tell us not to shed a single tear for him," said Mabel, though her tears were flowing profusely as she spoke.

"It is such a comfort to know Leonard was with him," said the mother. "He might have been left on the field, where we never could hear how he died or how much he suffered. That would have been terrible."

"Sydney was always ¡ . anxious to do good in some way," said Mabel; "and now he has been allowed to lay down his life for his country. I know it was a death he would have preferred to any other."

"Yes," replied the mother, "as grandfather used often to say, 'God never makes a mistake.' This mode of dying was the best mode, this time the best time. I haven't a doubt of it. My children were consecrated to God from their birth; and they are his, rather than mine, to dispose of as he chooses. He has done what seemeth good unto him, and I can say, 'Blessed be His name.'"

So, as the three sat around the fire that stormy night, though their tears were flowing, a sweet spirit of resignation, and even of thankfulness, pervaded the group. So doth God comfort his own in all time of tribulation.

A heavier gloom rested on their spirits when they thought of the country; for no personal loss could make their patriotic hearts insensible to the public calamity, and this reverse was most disheartening. Again Susan asked, "Has God forgotten to be gracious to us? Does he intend the destruction and ruin of our nation?" And again she fell back on the great, consoling truth that God was overruling all things, and that the great principles of right and freedom were forever safe in his keeping, however to a weak, finite vision they might seem imperilled.

"God is dealing with the nation as he deals with individuals," said Mrs. Roberts; "chastising us till we are made willing to forsake our sins and turn to him. But, as Leonard says, we must be as willing to trust our country in God's hands, as to trust ourselves."

"Sydney knows now how things look in the light of heaven," said Susan.

"Yes, and I can't help thinking grandfather would be the first to meet and welcome him there," said Mabel, "and to rejoice that he died for his country."

"It would seem so, judging from our present ideas," said Mrs. Roberts; "but we know so little of heaven that we cannot tell how things are there. We only know what the Bible tells us,—that it is a land of holiness, where nothing entereth in that defileth, and a land where 'there shall be no more death, neither sorrow nor crying, neither shall there be any more pain; for the former things are passed away.'"

A sweet, calm, heavenly brightness rested on the mother's face as she repeated the beautiful words of the Apocalypse; and both daughters knew that in her soul there was a hidden longing to go forth to that promised land, to be forever with the Lord. A new link to fasten her soul to heaven had been forged now; and, as she lay awake hour after hour that night, hearing the storm beat on the roof of the old red house, and thinking of her darling boy as a radiant spirit before the throne of God, her heart swelled with an unutterable emotion of gratitude to the Redeemer. With Mary of old, she could say, "My soul doth magnify the Lord, and my spirit hath rejoiced in God my Saviour."

In a few days, letters were received from Leonard, and also from the captain of Sydney's company and the chaplain of his regiment, each telling the bereaved mother of his bravery and nobleness, and of his labours in the camp and hospital. These tributes to his memory were the sweetest consolation the mother could have; and she felt that nothing but true worth could have won such appreciation and love as these letters showed.

"You may rest assured, dear madam," wrote the chaplain, "that your son, even in a short life, did much for his Master. More than one soul in this camp owed its faith in Christ to his exhortations and prayers; and none of our men will ever forget his earnest warnings and entreaties."

We give Leonard's letter in full:—

"You have before this heard, dear mother, that our beloved Sydney has gone: I know how it will grieve you; but, if you could have been with him at the last, you would have been comforted, as I was. I saw him two days before we crossed the river: he was in fine spirits, and said he had just written home. I never saw him looking in better health or handsomer. He was in a different division from mine, and after the battle it was a good while before I could get the least trace of him in the terrible confusion, and I had pretty much concluded he had been taken prisoner, when word was brought me that he was badly wounded and wanted me to come to him. He was shot through the left shoulder and side early in the action, and was carried to the rear and afterwards brought off among the other wounded. When I reached him, he was lying in an officer's tent, and had been kindly cared for. Surgeon K——, who loved him like a brother, had been with him; but the ball could not be extracted: he was suffering a good deal then, though much less than at first. It was about nine in the evening when I got to him. He knew me, and said, at once, 'This cannot last long, Leonard: I want to be patient while it does.' A heavy opiate was beginning to operate, and in about half an hour he sank into a sleep, troubled at first, but gradually growing deeper, till he lay as

## THE LAST SCENE.

calm and quiet as an infant. A little after midnight he woke up, and had one severe spasm of pain, and then slept again. About four in the morning he woke, free from pain, but so very weak he could not speak. I gave him wine, which revived him; and he talked at intervals both to me and to the surgeon, who looked in upon him occasionally, but could do nothing for him. 'He will not stand it many hours,' he whispered to me. Sydney heard him, and said, 'Then rest and heaven! I'm not afraid, you know,' he added, looking up pleasantly into my face, 'not at all afraid.' I prayed with him; when I ceased, he said, 'Oh, how good prayer is!' After a few minutes he said, in a whisper, 'Sing; sing *my* hymn.' At first I thought it would be impossible to utter a note; but he whispered again, as if he thought I was hesitating which hymn to sing, 'How sweet the name of Jesus sounds!' and I began and sang the whole hymn through,—that hymn we have all sung together so many times.

"As I went on, though his eyes were closed, the sweetest expression stole over his face,—an expression of perfect peace and trust. 'Thank you. How sweet!' he whispered. I repeated several passages of Scripture, and more than once he took up the words and finished the verse himself. Opening his eyes at one time, he said, 'Tell mother—' but he stopped, and seemed so drowsy that I did not like to rouse him. After sleeping a few minutes, he said, 'If mother only knew how comfortable I am here, she wouldn't grieve. Don't let her grieve,' he added, in a most affectionate tone. 'Tell her how easy I am,—oh, *so* easy!' He did not speak again for two hours; but about sunrise he roused, and, as I turned him in the bed, he asked, 'Is it morning?' 'Yes,' I said, 'the sun is just rising.' He smiled, and said, 'I thought I was in my own bed at home; but,' (looking round him,) 'how different it is!' Then, apparently remembering the battle and our retreat, he said, 'God will bring it all right.' 'Yes,' I replied, 'God loves our country still.' 'Yes, yes; oh, yes!' he answered, with much animation. After taking more wine, he lay back and said, with a sweet smile, 'I don't feel a pain; not one, tell mother and Mabel. They will think it is hard to die here; but it isn't. Christ is here, and that is enough. Yes, tell them,' he added, a moment after, 'that I had all I wanted.' There was a good deal of noise outside, and once it startled him, and he looked up as if disturbed; but in a moment he smiled, and said, 'The music of heaven,—the music of heaven!'

"'How sweet that will be!' I said. 'Yes, we shall all sing there, tell Susan,' remembering, I suppose, her regret that she could not join us here in singing. 'Tell them Christ stands close beside me. He is the resurrection and the life: there is no death!' These were his last words. He moved his head slightly, and a convulsion passed over his frame. Then there was a quick, laboured breathing for an hour or more, which gradually became shorter and fainter, and then ceased,—and your dear Sydney was with Christ in glory. '*There is no death!*' Oh, no, no death for him, nor for any who love Christ, who is the resurrection and the life! As I closed his eyes, a serene smile rested on the lips, as if he were just about to speak some pleasant thought. He lies under an oak-tree, and a board, with his name cut on it, marks the place. Here, on the soil of old Virginia, let your brave young soldier sleep! No purer or nobler spirit ever went up from her soil to God; and, among the thousands who have laid down their lives for their country, not one has done it from a nobler or higher motive than he. The very last words he said when we parted before the battle were, 'Leonard, we are glad we came!' The surgeon told me since his death that when he first went to him he said, 'You can't do any thing for me, doctor: don't waste time on me, when there are hundreds of poor fellows who want you so much more.' Yes, he was worthy of his name. Like Sydney of old, he would have taken the water from his own mouth to give to another dying soldier. You have a right to be proud of him, mother, and to rejoice in him, as one of a glorious company who,

> 'For God, for Truth, for Freedom's sake,
> Content the bitter cup to take,
> Have silently, in fearless faith,
> Bow'd down their noble souls to death,'

and whose blood shall not be spilt in vain. No, not in vain; for it shall surely buy for all coming generations untold blessings worthy of such a costly sacrifice. And the God of all comfort will draw nigh to you, dear mother, and comfort you. So certain am I of this, that I do not try to write consoling words, but only commit you to Him in faith. He will speak peace to your soul, and enable you to think less of your own sorrow than of the exceeding weight of glory of the saints above."

## CHAPTER XXIV.

### A SURPRISE.

In the red house, as in thousands of homes East and West during that memorable season, there were hearts that in the midst of desolation and bereavement called fervently on God. It would be far from true to say that in every family which had lost one of its members in the war, there was the solace of Christian faith and consolation; but into very many families Christ did come to strengthen and heal bleeding hearts. And, while there were sadness and tears and tender memories in such homes, there were no murmurs, no regrets at having given too much to the country; for in these homes there grew up a still stronger faith in God's overruling providence, and in the final success of the principles for which our people were so manfully contending.

It was beautiful to see how calmly Mrs. Roberts could speak of all her dear son had been to her, and look at all the old keepsakes left behind,—the memorials of his school and college days. It was not stoicism nor indifference, but a true, living faith in God and in his promise to raise the dead, which gave her this serenity. She never thought of Sydney as dead, but always as living a fuller and richer life than ever before,—never as under the sod in that far-off Virginian grave, but as in the city of the living God, among "the innumerable company of angels, and the general assembly and church of the first-born which are written in heaven." Of course, her heart often ached with an inexpressible longing to see his face once more, and to fold him to her heart; but the pang, though sharp, was short, and was soon lost in unselfish joy as she thought of his great gain.

Neighbours who came to see her, with

sad faces and words of tearful condolence, were astonished to find her face beaming with an inward peace and joy. Some wondered, and said, "How strange, not to feel her son's death more!" and their own faces grew still more sombre and gloomy. But those who knew her best knew the secret of her peace, and recognized it as the gift of God to a soul which had put its trust in him.

One day an old lady said to her, "Don't you feel sorry now that you let *both* your boys go to the war?"

She was almost startled at the energy with which the bereaved mother replied, "Sorry they have done all they could to save their country from dissolution! Sorry they are not traitors, nor cowards, nor selfish lovers of their own ease! Sorry that they have bravely stood up to protect the flag of the country that gave them birth, from those who would insult and degrade it! No, indeed. I do not think I could bear the defeats we have suffered, if I did not feel that I had given all I could to avert them. With a disgraced and divided country, how could I sit down with my sons around me and enjoy life? No! with that ruined, nothing else would be worth having,— nothing on earth! I pray God that if such is to be its end, he will be pleased to take me hence before it is accomplished!"

Leonard wrote every week, with less buoyancy of spirit than at first, yet he never permitted himself to doubt of the final result of the great conflict, again and again saying, "No, God isn't, *can't* be, on the side of treachery and oppression!" As furloughs were freely granted, he thought he might obtain one during the winter; but, having been recently raised to the rank of major, he could not at once release himself from duty, and dared not say when he should be willing to apply for leave of absence.

The very suggestion that he might come home filled his wife's heart with joy; but she would not allow herself to expect him; for a disappointment would be so very bitter.

One day in March, when the snow was melting from the roofs and the sugar-makers were just beginning to set their tubs under the maple-trees on the hill east of the red house, Uncle Roger took Susan and all the children for a day's visit to Grandmother Lee. The children were so excited they could hardly be kept quiet till they were packed into the sleigh. They had a charming ride of four miles, for Mrs. Lee lived in the opposite part of the town; and the glittering crust, the merry bells and the children's mirth made Susan almost as gleeful as the children themselves. She looked up to the cloudless sky, now taking on a softer tint of blue, and at the trees, brilliant with frost and ice, and said to herself, "This is a good world, after all, though there is so much sin and suffering in it." For a few days she had felt a little anxious at not having received her usual letter from her husband; but her fears passed off under those bright out-of-door influences, and she felt quite sure she should find a letter in the office when she came back at night.

Grandmother Lee's welcome was as hearty as the excited little folks could ask. Her stores of turn-overs, cookies and sugar gingerbread were as abundant, her pictures and toys kept tied up in a dark corner of her bedroom-closet were as funny and delightful as ever; and the dinner of stewed chicken, with apple-dumpling for dessert,—oh, where was such a dinner ever eaten,—where but at dear, good Grandmother Lee's? It was a day of rare enjoyment to them all; and, when they were bundled up in hoods and cloaks and comforters for the ride home, and grandmother had kissed each rosy little face and said they had been the best of children, they set off in great glee, more quiet than in the morning, but still very bright and happy.

No letter from the post-office! How strange it was! Could it be that a furlough had been given him and he was on his way home? Susan thought, in her heart, what if he were sick in the hospital, or even then lying lifeless on some little cot? The sun had gone, the air was chilly, the long gray shadows were creeping over the fields; and, somehow, the world seemed far less joyful and good than it did when she passed over that same road in the morning light. A presentiment of coming evil rested on her soul: had God sent it to prepare her for some terrible intelligence? Involuntarily she clasped Charlie closer to her breast, with a vague fear that he was fatherless, and sent up a prayer that she might be prepared for whatever tidings awaited her. She was calmer, and prepared, she thought, to bear any thing; but when, as she stepped out of the sleigh over the threshold of her own door, she was clasped in the arms of her husband, she shrieked, and almost fainted. No, she was not prepared for that; and Leonard almost blamed himself for not being more considerate, when she gave way to a flood of tears. But that was soon over, and she was conscious of the certainty of having her beloved husband once more at home, and of all the delight involved in it.

What exclamations of surprise and joy there were in the red house that night; what smiles and tears and tender memories; what narratives of strange adventures and wonderful escapes; what tributes of gratitude and thanksgiving; what petitions for the Lord's blessing on the country and its rulers, and what sweet communion of heart with heart, as, later, they sat together, the true husband and the faithful wife, by their own home fireside, it were useless to try to tell. Verily, if war has its hours of woe and horror, it has also its hours of rare delight. Without the pain and the agony they had endured, there could never have come a joy so thrilling, so rich and full, as they experienced now.

The furlough was for twenty days, and several of these must be consumed in coming and returning. It really seemed as if his family saw very little of "the major," as he was called; for the neighbours crowded around him eager for information, as all of them, or nearly all, had some friend in Virginia, either in the army or in the grave. To their inquiries Leonard listened patiently; and he went more than once to see the widows of the two brave soldiers who had fallen in the same battle with Sydney, and whom he had seen carefully buried by his side. To these he gave words of cheer and hope, and commended them in prayer to the compassion and tender mercy of their God and Saviour.

Leonard was a good deal changed in person, and somewhat in manner; but he was the same quiet, thoughtful man as formerly, taking calm and sensible views of things. He was still hopeful as to the final result of the war, though not enthusiastic as to the immediate success of our arms.

"I fear it may be a long war," he said, one evening, as he sat conversing with several neighbours, among whom was his old friend Judge Bailey. It was a dark hour then. With the enemy successful in the field, and foreign nations unkindly disposed, or about, as many feared, to recognize the Confederacy, and the home-elections showing divisions among ourselves, there was cause enough for despondency and doubt; and in all our villages people were saying, just as one of the group remarked in reply to Leonard, "Yes, and I doubt if we shall keep our country together, after all. Here we are, at the end of two years, just as far as ever from putting down the rebellion; and what thousands of lives have been sacrificed,— yes, sacrificed in vain, I fear! I begin to think God means to destroy us for our wickedness."

"Possibly he does," answered Leonard. "We can't know God's plans. We only know we must do our duty, and keep alive our faith in him. For myself, I don't by any means give up hope of our final success. We are strong still in men and resources of all kinds, but infinitely stronger in the justice of our cause. For one, I have no idea that injustice and wrong are going to prevail. We may have even worse reverses than we have experienced yet; but I believe we shall yet see our Union firmer and stronger than it ever was before."

"So do I," said Judge Bailey. "One great trouble is, we are too impatient and hasty. No great question is settled in a hurry; and when I think what lasting issues are involved in this war, I feel pretty certain they can't be settled in one year, or in two. They may not be in ten. I know as a people we are given to exaggeration, but it is no figure of speech to say the whole world is interested in these questions and will be affected by their decision."

"Well, judge, I wish you'd tell us what you think are the great points to be settled," said Mr. Hall, a farmer, who had two sons in the army. "You are a thinking man, and can put things into shape; and, I must say, I get a good deal puzzled myself in thinking these things over."

"I can only tell you how they appear to my own mind, Mr. Hall; and, I take it, the wisest men in the country are puzzled in these days, as well as you. But there are some principles which I think are involved in this contest that all can understand. They don't all lie on the surface, though; and therefore we may lose sight of them at times. The apparent question to be settled, we all know, is, Has a State a right to withdraw from the Union? That will be decided now, one way or another, for all the future. This is a great question, and a vital one to our own nation. But there are others, much more important, and in which other nations are interested. One of them is, whether a republic can sustain itself in a great emergency? Foreign nations scoff at us, and say, 'No. As soon as any trouble comes, you see, such a government shows itself to be weak and powerless. It must be so,' because 'Republics are weak from their very nature. They have nothing but the people to lean upon; and the people are always fickle, restless and clamorous, and sure to give way just at the time when strength and firmness are wanted. You'll see how they'll quarrel among themselves, find fault with their rulers and officers, and break up into parties. And there is no central force at Washington strong enough to combine these elements and wield them to any purpose. You'll see that no government by the people can carry a nation through a civil war. It will fail. There isn't a doubt of it. It's a foregone conclusion.'

"Yes, a government by the people—in other words, a republican form of government—is on trial before the world; and the world is looking on to see the result. And it seems as if Providence, determined it should be a thorough trial and made on a grand scale, has let this war spread out into gigantic dimensions, in order that nothing should be wanting in the test. A wider extent of territory is involved than in any war the world has ever seen, more men are in the field, and more treasure lavished on it. As I say, the men in power in the Old World are sure we shall fail; but the people there know it isn't settled yet, and they stand watching with eager eyes to see whether we are really to be ruined or not; whether there is, indeed, no hope of free institutions existing anywhere on the earth. If they fail in America, the people of other countries, who have been hoping to rise to some share in their own government, will sink back in despair. We have asserted that the people are competent to rule themselves, and can be trusted to do it. Now we are to make good this boast. If we do prove it, the way will be opened for the advancement of free institutions in other nations; if we fail, their hopes fail too."

"Well, I hadn't thought of it in this way exactly, I own," said Mr. Hall; "but I guess you are about right. I guess the rulers over there do feel some interest in the settlement of our affairs."

"Doubtless they do," said Leonard; "but the people feel more. In almost every country in Europe there is a movement towards greater freedom among the masses; a feeling that they have rights which are not recognized by their governments; and they are the most interested in the fate of the only republic they know much about."

"It's a gigantic question, and, as I said before, if we don't see it settled in a hurry, we must be patient," said Judge Bailey. "The Germans have a proverb, 'God's mills grind very slowly, but they grind very fine.'*

"Another great question to be solved," continued he, "is whether African slavery is to be an enduring institution. If the South succeed, slavery will have a new lease of life. They profess to believe, perhaps some honestly think, that slavery is the proper condition of the African, the one God intended him for; that man has a right to buy and sell and rule over his fellow-man of another race and colour; and they contend that society thus organized is the best phase of social life, pleasing to God and beneficial to man. The people of the North believe the reverse. They believe that this system, entailed on the South not so much perhaps by their own fault as by the force of circumstances, is

---

* Longfellow's rendering of this proverb is,—
"Though the mills of God grind slowly, yet they grind
    exceeding small;
Though with patience he stands waiting, with exactness
    grinds he all."

a system of wrong and outrage, blighting every country where it has existed, and proving a curse as well to the master as the slave. They regard it as a relic of the dark ages, which, in the progress of Christian principles, must be done away with; and they think that this war, inaugurated by the South for the extension of the system, is likely, in God's hands, to prove its ruin. At least, we all believe that the issue of this war will have a direct bearing on the institution, and the world is looking on to see how this problem will be solved. So let us remember that we are not fighting merely for our own interests, but for principles which affect all nations; and if we only prove true to ourselves, I believe they will all be adjusted in such a way as to advance the great cause of human rights over the whole world. I believe this, because God overrules all events, and because he has caused steady progress to be made towards freedom and knowledge in the past."

"Yes," he added, after a pause in which

no one spoke, "it is this hope which carries me through the trials of these times. I am an old man and long for quiet, but I hope I long for freedom and righteousness more. When I think of our country as once more all one, with the great cause of discord and division done away, having everywhere through all its length and breadth free labour and free schools, enlightened communities and prosperous churches, I am reconciled to God's bringing about this great result even by such a fearful war as this."

"It warms up a body's heart to take this view of the case," said Mr. Hall; "and I hope it will all come true."

"But we must all do our duty in order to have it come true," said Leonard. "It won't do to become faint-hearted in the very midst of the conflict. Our government must rely on the people to carry it through; and if they do their duty all will be well. God will help us if we help ourselves. I confess my great fear is that this generation may not prove itself worthy of this opportunity, and so lose the glory of bringing about these grand results."

"Then the ground must be all gone over again, by those who come after us," said the judge, "till a generation is found that is worthy and can persevere to the end. But I believe God means they should be accomplished now, and that he will give us courage enough and faith enough to hold out till a peace is secured based on right principles, and which will be lasting."

After they parted, and the judge was seated by his own fireside, he said to his wife, "That Leonard Roberts is a brave fellow. He has improved very much, and he always was an uncommon boy."

"Yes, he was," replied his wife. "He was always so honest, and so careful to do exactly right, I was sure he would make a noble man."

"Yes, it's that trying to do right that really makes a man, after all. Leonard carries it into every thing now. I like his views about the war. He goes below the surface. He knows what we are fighting for, and why our institutions are valuable and worth sustaining. He is a very intelligent man, too. I can't conceive how he came to know so much; for he couldn't have had many advantages in early life."

"No; but he was a great reader. Instead of spending all his evenings at the store, or in playing with other boys, he stayed at home and read; and I've heard his mother say he never forgot any thing he read: so now he has a fund of knowledge ready for use."

"Well, I feel proud to think that such a man has grown up here in Woodlee. Sydney was more of a scholar, but I doubt if he had the substantial good sense Leonard has."

"He was a bright, charming boy, though. It was a dreadful thing to have him die there; but Mrs. Roberts bore it heroically."

"Rather like the good Christian woman that she is," said the judge; "and Leonard is a Christian, too. It's his religion makes him what he is,—truly brave and loyal."

"But a great many men are loyal who are not religious."

"Perhaps so, in a certain way; but not in the highest sense of the word. Leonard is loyal to his country because he believes God requires him to be, and that he is serving God while he serves his country. His religion includes his loyalty, as the greater contains the less; and loyalty becomes an inspiration to a man when he bases it on his obligations to God. And all loyalty not thus based is comparatively poor and weak."

"I hope Leonard will be spared," said Mrs. Bailey. "It must be very hard for his family to have him go back again."

"Yes, but his family are loyal too, and loyal after the same pattern. They love their country and make sacrifices for it because they believe God requires it. They are an example of what a Christian family should be in times like these. They deserve to stand by the side of the mothers and wives of the Revolution; and they do, I am sure, in God's sight."

"And a host of other wives and mothers."

"Yes, I am proud of the women of the North: God bless them, and give them strength to endure unto the end!" said the old gentleman, fervently, as he leaned back in his chair.

## CHAPTER XXV.

### THE PARTING.

Leonard's short visit soon drew to a close, and the last evening of his stay had come. Susan sat by the table, sewing together the leaves of the little Bible which he carried in his pocket,—the one his grandfather gave him in his boyhood, and which had once belonged to Gilbert Watson, who died at sea. It looked very ancient now; but, tattered and soiled as it was, it was far more precious to Leonard than any modern one.

"Somehow, this little Bible always brings home nearer to me than any thing else," said he; "and, when I take it out by the camp-fire, a thousand tender thoughts come with it. It takes me back to my childhood, and I hear again dear grandfather's voice, and the rustle of the leaves in the chestnut-trees, just as I did when I sat down by my window in the red house to read a chapter out of it. I was very much touched at the time by grandfather's account of the sick lad who gave him this Bible; and when he gave it to me, I remember, I made a solemn resolution to read it every day, and to try to learn from it my duty to God and to myself. Grandfather said it had taught him the way of salvation; and I was sure it could teach me. Yes, it has been a blessed book,—first to the invalid boy who used to sit by himself in one corner of the deck and read it, then to the thoughtless sailor to whom he bequeathed it, and now to me. What strange scenes it has witnessed! And it may witness stranger yet; for I always keep it with me. When we were on the eve of our first battle, I took it out and turned to the passage dear grandfather had marked with his trembling hand,—'*The Lord bless thee, and keep thee; the Lord make his face shine upon thee, and be gracious unto thee; the Lord lift up his countenance upon thee, and give thee peace.'* 'This is what I wish for you, my boy,' he said: I remember perfectly how he looked as he said it; and I felt sure, among all the confusion of that camp, that God's blessing did descend directly upon me. Yes, Susan, God has blessed me all my life. He has always 'crowned me with loving-kindness and tender mercy;' and I know he will continue to bless me still."

"Many would think such a life as your's a hard one," said Susan: " it has certainly been full of hard work and care from the first, and now it is not only full of hardship, but danger too."

"I know it; but it is a life I wouldn't exchange for one of ease and luxury. I like to feel that I am living to some purpose,—living like a man! The night I was twenty-one, I stood by that little attic window in the old red house and looked out on the stars, and asked God to help me to make my life of some value to myself and others. How well I remember it! My life has been a poor one, compared to what I hoped then; but I can honestly say I have looked to God for direction in all the important events of it. And he has answered—yes, and more than answered—my requests. He has always guarded and guided me like a tender father; and, even when things have gone wrong outwardly, he has given me a great deal of inward peace and joy. Now, Susan, let what will come, I can trust him. I may be poor, or sick, or die away from home, but I know he will never forsake me, no matter where I am or how much I may suffer."

Susan's tears flowed freely, but inward peace and strength were in her heart. On some accounts, it was harder to part with her husband now than at first; but she had not grown weaker in the furnace of affliction, and she was now more convinced that sacrifices must be made, than even in the first year of the war. The hand had been put to the plough, and there must be no looking back till the great work was done which should restore our country to peace, unity and liberty.

"One trial I have never had," said Leonard, smiling, "so I can't tell how I could bear that:—the trial of a weak-minded, selfish wife, who was drawing me back from my duty all the while."

Susan looked up, and smiled through her tears.

"Thousands of times," said her husband, "when I have been inclined to fret about something, I have thought of your smile, and said to myself, 'She is having a harder time than I; but I know she is making the best of it.' It must be dreadful for a soldier to know his wife at home is fretting and complaining all the time. It must do a good deal to take the courage out of him. But I never think of mine without feeling stronger for every duty."

The next morning, before daylight, Leonard had gone ; the last embrace had been given, the last "God bless you!" uttered, and the soldier was on his way to the camp once more. Things soon settled down into the old routine at the red house, and letters came as before from Leonard, telling of his safe arrival at head-quarters, and of his being once more occupied with the duties of his station.

There we must leave him. What the changes and chances of war may bring to him, we cannot foretell ; only of this we can rest assured, that he will be sustained through all those changes by a living faith in God, and will prove himself truly loyal, not only to the country he has sworn to defend against all her foes, but also to the God of nations. For this we could have no better guaranty than his past life. He who in his childhood was loyal to his parents, and in youth and manhood loyal to his conscience and his God, cannot prove false or traitorous, in his later years, to his country or to his duty as a man or Christian. He will be upheld by an almighty arm; and, whether his life shall be prolonged to a quiet old age among his native hills, or be cut short on the battle-field or in the hospital, he has the promise of God that "it shall be well with him, and with his children after him."

Neither can we foresee what the great current of events, now sweeping rapidly onward and presenting new problems to the thoughtful mind with each passing month, shall bring to our beloved land; but we may rest assured that the great interests of humanity are safe in the keeping of our God. We know his cause shall prosper, and that his cause is the cause of human rights and human progress,—the cause of truth, of freedom, of justice,—those eternal attributes of his throne which nothing can destroy, and which shall at last everywhere prevail. To this eternal, unchangeable, infinite Being, who sitteth in the heavens, lifted up far above all dimness and doubt, all discord and tumult, watching with serene eye the warfares waging on earth, and controlling the destiny of nations, we commend our country in this hour of conflict, praying that out of all this seeming evil he will educe good, and from this fearful baptism of blood and fire bring her forth purified and redeemed, and made worthy to spread, throughout the world, the knowledge of God and of the principles which support his throne and which alone can give stability to human governments. Consecrated by its founders to liberty and piety, may it yet live to do a high and holy work for God among the nations, and see fulfilled in its own experience the promise of God to his people of old:—"I will make them one nation in the land; and they shall be no more two nations: neither shall they defile themselves any more with their transgressions: but I will save them, and will cleanse them: so shall they be my people, and I will be their

God. And they shall walk in my judgments, and observe my statutes, and do them. And they shall dwell in the land, even they, and their children, and their children's children forever; and I will set my sanctuary in the midst of them for evermore."

THE END.

www.ingramcontent.com/pod-product-compliance
Lightning Source LLC
Chambersburg PA
CBHW020304240426
43673CB00039B/696